FOLK TALES OF SIND AND GUZARAT

FOLK TALES OF SIND AND GUZARAT

C. A. KINCAID

GYAN

Published by

GYAN

Gyan Publishing House
5, Ansari Road
Daryaganj, New Delhi-110002
Phone: 011-47034999, 9811692060
E-mail: books@gyanbooks.com

Distribution Network
gyanbooks.com
India, USA, Canada, UK, Australia, France

ISBN : 978-81-212-3385-9 (PB)
First Published, 1925

2nd Impression 2020

Printed at: Gyan Press, Delhi.

Folk Tales of Sind and Guzarat
Author: C. A. Kincaid

FOLK TALES OF SIND AND GUZARAT

BY

C. A. KINCAID, C.V.O., I.C.S.
Officie de l'Instruction Publique.

THE DAILY GAZETTE PRESS, LTD.,
KARACHI.

1925.

To

JEAN LOUIS RIEU, C. S. I., I. C. S.,

Commissioner-in-Sind.

this book is inscribed in memory of an unclouded and greatly valued friendship lasting for over thirty years.

'Satan is the only true lover, all others are mere prattlers. Out of his great love for his Lord, the shining one (Satan) incurred disgrace."

SHAH LATIF.

Commentator.—God needed opposition to make Him realise His almighty strength. To give God full possession of it, Satan sacrificed himself and rebelled, although he knew that he would thereafter be punished eternally.

AUTHOR'S PREFACE.

Most of the articles collected in this little book have appeared in the "Daily Gazette" or the "Times of India." They are reprinted with the kind permission of the Editors. I do not claim for them any merit beyond the fact that they touch the fringe of an unexplored country. My hope is that they will lead others more competent than I am and with greater opportunities than I have had, to delve into the vast treasures of folklore possessed by the Province of Sind.

The four Guzarati stories have been added, because although they come from a different part of India, they are still folk tales and belong to the same category as the Sind tales. I am indebted to Mr. Amritlal Chunilal, Vakil of Kapadwanj, for the originals of the Guzarati stories.

C. A. K.

FOREWORD.

Be the fact good or bad for the Province, fact it is. The beauties of Sind are not for the stranger, or casual visitor. He, perhaps merely seeking the shortest and quickest route to some temporary post up North, or possibly to his permanent home in the damp, grey West, notices only torrid heat, arid wastes, blinding glare, suffocating dust, and a coastal Port somewhat reminiscent of Suez or Port Said. Not for him the enchanting views from the little islands at Bhukkar, or from the banks of the lower reaches of the Indus below Hyderabad. Not for him the green grain fields and shady forests that fringe the great river between Larkana and the late Capital. Not for him the scent of the old Kumbar Road, or the myriad bird life of the Munchar Lake. Not for him the moonlight on the great desert on our Eastern frontier; or the sunrise from the Indus delta, throwing its golden shafts across Karachi's beautiful lagoon to the rugged sky-line of the Hub hills.

But for the old Sindhi these things mean much. Further, nobody who has lived long in Sind, can have failed to be affected not only by its beauties, but by the atmosphere of romance that pervades the whole Province. It meets one on every side —north, south, east and west. But little imagination is required to picture the argosies of bygone centuries sailing silently down the river past the green fields of Kushmore: or the old caravans from Kandahar with their strings of stately camels slowly emerging from the foot of the Bolan Pass on their way to Shikarpur: or the *buggalas* of old Nearchus nestling in the Chinna Creek in the shelter of the Oyster Rocks during the monsoon, patiently awaiting the arrival of the Great Alexander shortly to appear at the Ghizree mouth of the Indus on the conclusion of his triumphal progress through Western Asia! Then, too, think of the circumstances leading up to the birth at Oomerkot of that infant who was afterwards to be one of the greatest rulers in Indian history,—the mighty Akbar. Here are materials for romances galore.

We are not dependent, however, simply on historical incidents to stimulate our imaginations. Though the vagaries of the Indus and the severity of the hot season in the interior combine quickly to obliterate man's puny strivings for permanency, material evidence exists in many places of the great vitality and culture of those who have lived before us in this ancient land of Sind. The beautifully coloured and perfectly glazed tiles and pottery of Hala bear testimony to an art lost to the present generation of Sindhis; whilst the ornamented graves and temples which can still be seen in many parts of the Province, reveal the existence in the past of a God-fearing people with well developed notions of sculpture and architecture. Who can regard the wonderful tombs on the Makli Hill at Tatta or the ruins of the great city of Brahminabad without realising that those responsible for these things must have been, in their day, well advanced in social and civilised life, and deserving of the respect of the present generation.

It is about certain leaders—religious and political—of these peoples of the bygone centuries that the Hon. Mr. Justice Kincaid has compiled the stories that have been reproduced in the following pages. The stories which have been passed on from generation to generation, are, like the legends of the West, to some extent mythical, but no doubt based on actual incidents in the past which, in the repeated telling, have been added to and embroidered in a way calculated to impress the minds of the simple folk who heard them ; and thus their remembrance and transmission to later generations has been assured. Mr. Kincaid has well caught the spirit of the stories, and his transcriptions are in his happiest style. The thanks of every patriotic Sindhi will go out to him for thus preserving in the printed page the legends that have grown up around some of the more celebrated figures and remains of ancient Sind.

But we hope that Mr. Kincaid's good work will not cease yet. The investigations of the Archaeological Department of the Government of India have recently brought to light facts that have turned the eyes of the whole world towards the valley of the Indus. Searching amongst the ruins of northern Sind, Mr. Rakhaldas Bannerji has discovered at Mohenjo Daro in the Larkana District buildings and domestic articles that seem to indicate the existence in Sind of an advanced civilisation some thousands of years ago ! This discovery is confirmed by the unearthing, almost at the same time, of similar remains 400 miles away at Harappa in the Montgomery District of the Punjab. These remains include " houses and temples, massively built of burnt brick, and provided with well constructed water conduits covered with marble slabs. The smaller antiquities include a quantity of pottery—painted and plain, terra cotta, toys, bangles of blue glass, paste and shell, new types of coins (or tokens), curious stone rings and dice." Further, there are a number of engraved and inscribed seals bearing inscriptions in a hitherto unknown pictographic script. A careful comparison has now confirmed the surmise that these antiquities are closely connected and contemporary with the Sumerian antiquities of southern Mesopotamia, dating from the third or fourth millenium before Christ. And so the conclusion has been arrived at that the peoples of Sind and the Punjab were living in "well-built cities in a relatively mature civilisation with a high standard of art and craftmanship and a developed system of writing 5,000 years ago." (*vide* Sir John Marshall, Director-General of Archaeology in India's communications to the *Pioneer* and to the *Times* in November and December, 1924).

Whether any trace of this remote civilisation can be detected in any of the old legends at present current among the country-folk of Sind, it is impossible to say. We hope that Mr. Kincaid will be able to continue his investigations into these matters, and will give to the public all that he can find. With the translation of the pictographic script on the recently discovered seals, some clue or connection with later civilisations may possibly be traced. A fascinating vista of Sind, *i.e.*, the land of the Indus, as the cradle of modern Civilisation has been opened up, (for Sumerian culture was probably the source of Babylonian, Assyrian and Western Asiatic culture). It is to be hoped that the Government of India will continue its investigations with redoubled energy, and will further explore the rich plains on both banks of the Indus.

M. DE P. WEBB.

London, 16th December, 1924.

CONTENTS.

I.—SIND FOLK STORIES.

II.—GUZARAT FOLK STORIES.

III.—ROUND ABOUT NASIK.

FOLK TALES OF SIND AND GUZARAT.

LAL SHAHBAZ.

A SIND SAINT.

Sehwan is known to Englishmen chiefly as a handy station for those who wish to shoot on the Manchar lake. In the summer it enjoys an unenviable reputation for heat. The bare rocks of Lakhi known as the Bagothoro are said to end the last struggles of the monsoon. Indeed the Lakhi pass is known locally as the gate of the infernal regions; and an often quoted Persian couplet about Sehwan runs as follows:

"When both Sehwan and Sibi grill so well
What good was there, O Lord, in making Hell?" *

But besides its fame as a sporting and a roasting centre, Sehwan has an immense reputation for sanctity. Within its confines repose in mighty state the earthly remains of the greatest saint of all Sind, worshipped alike by Musulmans and Hindus, the renowned Lal Shahbaz, the Red Peregrine Falcon of the Indus valley.

Lal Shahbaz's real name was Hazrat Sayad Usman Shah Marwandi. He was born at Marwand in Afghanistan in A. H. 538. His father Makhdum Sayad Ahmed Kabir was a powerful noble and a great friend of the king of Tabriz. From his earliest years, so it is said, the boy shewed a great leaning towards things spiritual. Before his twelfth year he had already made the blind see, the deaf hear and the dumb speak. When Lal Shahbaz reached manhood, he insisted on leaving his father's house and started on a pilgrimage. He first went to Baghdad

---

The Persian runs :—*Shiristan o Sibi Sakhti chira dozakh pardakhti.

where he stayed at the court of the monarch Sayad Ali. When he wished to leave, Sayad Ali implored him to remain at Baghdad for ever. But the religious call was too insistent and with three friends, Sheikh Bahawaldin, Sheikh Farid Ganj Shakar and Makhdum Jalaluddin, Lal Shahbaz set off for the Persian Gulf. In an island in the Gulf lived a fakir named Sheikh Jalal whose austerities had won him supernatural gifts. Lal Shahbaz determined to reduce him to obedience and make him his disciple. No boats were available so Lal Shahbaz threw his "kishta" or begging bowl into the water and it became a boat. Into it the four friends stepped and rowed for Sheikh Jalal's island. About half way the boat stopped dead and no matter how hard the saints plied the oar, it declined to move. At last Lal Shahbaz realised that the island fakir had cast a spell on them. But he could only have done that, if one among them was not a true anchorite and was still thinking of the joys of this world, while pretending to have given them up for ever. Lal Shahbaz told this to his friends and asked them whether they had one and all given up the world wholly. They protested their complete unworldliness. But as the boat still refused to budge, Lal Shahbaz went through their pockets. In the pocket of Sheikh Bahawaldin he found, as I regret to say, a brick of solid gold, which the saint was keeping against a rainy day. Lal Shahbaz threw it overboard. Once freed from this sordid freight, the boat began again to move. As they drew near the island, Lal Shahbaz saw Sheikh Jalal looking at them through a window of his castle. To punish him for stopping the boat, Lal Shahbaz made the window grow so small that it gripped the fakir's neck as if in a vice. Sheikh Jalal yelled for mercy, but it was not granted him until he had owned himself beaten and had promised to become an obedient and humble follower of Lal Shahbaz.

The great saint acquired his appellation of Lal Shahbaz, by two remarkable miracles. After the defeat of Sheikh Jalal, Lal Shahbaz and his three companions went to Mecca and Medina. As they were returning from the blessed vision of the prophet's tomb, they halted one night in a town on the coast of Arabia. Sheikh Farid Shakar Ganj went to buy bread for the party. Unhappily the baker's wife conceived an unholy passion for the young man. Like a true ascetic he rejected her odious advances with the icy disdain of Saint Joseph. The baker's wife thereupon behaved after the manner of Potiphar's consort. She began to scream that Sheikh Farid Shakar Ganj had tried to outrage her. The unhappy anchorite was seized, dragged before the governor and condemned to instant execution. Lal Shahbaz heard of it and took immediate steps to rescue his innocent friend. He changed one of his two remaining friends into a deer and bade him run towards the gallows. The crowd ran madly after the deer to catch it. Lal Shahbaz turned his second friend into a lion. It charged the executioners roaring terribly. They fled incontinently. Lastly the Saint changed himself into a peregrine falcon and swooping down picked up Sheikh Farid Shakar Ganj and bore him to a place of safety. By this miracle the Saint got the name o Shahbaz, the Sindhi word for a peregrine falcon. How did he obtain the title of Lal? It was this way: A certain Murshid once challenged Shahbaz's friends to bathe in a caldron of boiling oil. They not unnaturally declined the challenge, whereupon the Murshid mocked them as unworthy impostors. They sorrowfully told their master of their discomfiture. On the instant he accepted the challenge and going to the Murshid's house leapt into the boiling oil. He stayed so long at the bottom of the cauldron that his rival owned himself beaten. "Come out," he cried, "you are indeed a Lal among Lals (a ruby among rubies)". The master rose triumphantly out of the oil. He had suffered no harm from the immersion, but the heat of the oil had turned his robe crimson. That robe he wore to his dying day and was in the end buried in it. So he came to be known as Lal Shahbaz.

After his journey to Mecca and Medina, Lal Shahbaz came to Sind. He wandered until he came to a spot still called 'Lal jo Bagh' or the garden of the ruby, two miles from Sehwan. Sehwan was, however, already a holy town and its worldly minded fakirs dreaded that the advent of so famous a mendicant would reduce their earnings. They sent him a cup full to the brim of milk, that he might know that just as the cup could hold no more milk, so Sehwan could hold no more anchorites. Lal Shahbaz sent to those worldly minded ones a fitting answer. He made a flower float on the milk and returned the cup, thereby shewing to the fakirs that there was still room for yet another holy man and that the newcomer meant to be above the others, even as the flower was above the milk. After this event Lal Shahbaz spent most of his time in Sehwan. His friend Sheikh Bahawaldin left him and went to Multan. Before leaving he offered to Lal Shahbaz and the latter accepted the hand of his daughter. Not long afterwards Lal Shahbaz learnt in a trance of the death of his prospective father-in-law. He went to Multan and asked Sheikh Bahawaldin's son, Sadaruddin for his betrothed. Sadaruddin refused. The Saint thereupon cursed him and vowed that the girl should wed no one else, but would find an instant resting place in paradise. Shortly afterwards the poor girl died and Lal Shahbaz returned to Sehwan. He died on the 21st of the month of Shaban 650 A. H. at the ripe age of 112; and the anniversary of his death is kept as a great festival. From all quarters of Sind come fakirs and musicians and dancing girls to dance before the shrine of the mighty anchorite. The chief feature of the celebration is the marriage of Lal Shahbaz to his lost bride.

Now why do Hindus worship at his shrine ? That is perhaps the strangest part of the story. In 56 B. C. lived the great king Vikramaditya of Dharmanagar or Ujjain, the Arthur of Hindu historical legends. At his court lived the nine gems of learning and his valour and his arms reduced all India to subjection. Once upon a time he resolved to disguise himself and see with his own eyes how his viceroys governed his provinces. He appointed to be his regent during his absence his younger brother Brartrahari. One day the Goddess Parvati gave to a devout old couple in Ujjain an apple, that conferred immortality on anyone who ate it. The old couple preferring riches to immortality sold the apple to the regent for a great price. The regent gave it to his youngest and prettiest wife. She unfortunately had a lover and she gave the apple to him. He in turn presented it to a dancing girl, who sold it back to Brartrahari. The regent thereby discovered his wife's infidelity. In a rage he flung away the apple and abandoning his office, became an anchorite. According to the local legend, he wandered until he came to Sind, where he became a devoted worshipper of Shiva. He called his abiding place Shivisthan or the place of Shiva. From Shivisthan has come the modern name Sehwan. Brartrahari lived at Sehwan until he died and by his life and death made the spot holy. The Musulman invasion swept away the temple of Shiva, but the memory of the pious recluse lingered on ; and when Lal Shahbaz came and worked miracles at the spot where Brartrahari had lived, the Hindus declared that Lal Shahbaz was his reincarnation.

The miraculous powers of Lal Shahbaz did not die with him. After his death streams of molasses, sugar and milk are said to have spurted from the wall of his tomb. These articles he meant for the use of the poor of Sehwan only. Nor did he mean that any should take more than one helping in any one day. Sad to relate, his pious wishes were brought to nought by the greed of the townspeople. Poor and rich alike rushed to profit by the dead saint's bounty and none confined himself to a single helping. In disgust the dead saint bade the streams dry up and all that now remains of them is a group of stones that look exactly like petrified sugar molasses and milk. These the guardians of the shrine shew to wondering pilgrims as proof positive of the legend's truth.

UDERO LAL.

Udero Lal was born on Cheti Chand, the first day of the Sindhi month Cheti and also the first day of what is known as the Chaitradi year—the year that begins with the month of Cheti or Chaitra instead of the month of Kartak. In Udero Lal's honour the Government offices throughout Sind are closed. So in common gratitude every Government officer ought to enquire who Udero Lal was. He was the son of an aged couple called Ratno and Devki, who lived at Nasarpur. Ratno hawked cooked gram and was a devout worshipper of the Indus river. They had two sons already, but had long passed the age when married couples hope for more children. Ratno was sixty and Devki over forty, when Udero Lal was born. But Udero Lal's birth was due to divine interposition. The cause of it was as follows :—

In the year 939 A. D. one Marak was governor of Tatta. He was a bigoted Musulman and he suddenly resolved to convert to Islam the whole Hindu population under him. He proclaimed by beat of drum, that he would kill every Hindu, who did not change his faith within twenty-four hours. So alarmed were the Hindus that, so the story runs, all their cooking pots fell from their shelves ; and exclaiming that a camel had entered the king's head*, they went in a body to his minister Aho. Through him they gained a fortnight's respite. At that time, so the legend has it, the Indus flowed past Tatta. On its banks the despairing Hindus gathered and prayed to the great river to save them from the hands of Marak. At the same time they vowed that if no answer was vouchsafed to their prayers within a week, they would throw their children into the stream. On the fourteenth day they would with their wives in their arms throw themselves into it and thus escape the cruelty of Marak.

On the seventh day when they were on the point of drowning all their babies, they saw the river god himself rise from the waves, a beautiful figure, all of snow-white foam. He bade the Hindus no longer despair. He had heard their supplications and within the allotted fortnight he would be born in the house of Ratno, the gram hawker. He bade them warn Marak of his approaching birth. They did so and the wicked governor sent Aho to seize the baby directly it was born. The child Udero Lal arrived on the last day of the fortnight. Aho was about to seize it, when it changed instantly into a youth of sixteen, then into an old man and once more into an infant. Aho was dumbfounded and his hatred and unbelief changed to love and faith. He begged the child to return with him to Marak, so as to convince him also. The babe replied " Go back to Tatta. There stand on the banks of the Indus and call me and I shall come."

Aho went back to Tatta and told Marak. The governor was frightened out of his wits, still he ordered Aho to go to the river bank and call on Udero Lal to rise from the river. Aho did so and as the words left his lips, a tall beautiful youth, riding

i.e. *That he had gone mad.

a noble steed, rose from the river and behind him followed thousands of soldiers and horsemen, chariots and war elephants. The terrified minister fell at Udero Lal's feet and begged him to send away the mighty army that followed in his footsteps. The youth turned round and dismissed his warriors. A moment later the great army had vanished into the depths of the Indus. Aho led Udero Lal into Marak's presence and told him the marvels that he had witnessed. Marak instantly seated Udero Lal on his right hand and craved his advice. Udero Lal bade him to cease from his cruelty to his Hindu subjects. But while Marak listened with pious looks to Udero Lal's words, his heart was full of black treachery. After he had escorted with all reverence the beautiful youth to one of his palaces, he ordered his soldiers to surround it. For he now plotted to convert to Islam not only his Hindu subjects but Udero Lal also. But it was idle to strive to bind the Indus river. When the kazi and the surgeon came to convert him he had vanished.

The indignant Marak resolved not to give his Hindu subjects a day's more grace and announced that he would convert or kill them all that very evening. They went to Ratno's house. There they found Udero Lal, once more a baby in the cradle. They prayed to the divine child and he bade them go to the river and sit in a temple that they would find there. When all the Hindus had assembled, a fearful thunderstorm burst and fire from heaven consumed the palace of the governor and the houses of his officers. Marak, Aho and the kazi, although badly burnt, escaped from the conflagration and ran to the river. There they saw a splendid temple and in it were seated Udero Lal, once more a beautiful youth and round him thousands of Hindus, perfectly sheltered from the storm that had fallen on Tatta. The three wicked men fell at Udero Lal's feet and Marak took a mighty oath never again to harass the Hindus. Udero Lal then bade the winds be still and the storm at once passed away. Udero Lal vanished and so did the magic temple. But the Hindus built on the spot a real one of stone that stands to this day. Lights burn in it day and night and it is known as the Khudio temple or the temple of Refuge.

When the Hindus went to Nasarpur to tell Ratno and Devki how their child had helped them, they found Udero Lal once more a baby sleeping peacefully in his cradle. Nothing further happened until Udero Lal was a little boy of six, when his mother Devki thought that he might help his father by hawking cooked gram too. She gave him a tiny jar of cooked gram and bade him hawk it through the streets of Nasarpur, taking payment either in cash or in kind. That evening Udero Lal brought back a huge pot full of grain and gave it to his mother. This went on for several days until his parents grew more and more curious to know how he got grain many times its value for the cooked gram. Next day they followed him and they saw their little son go to the river bank and dip the jar of cooked gram into the water. When he pulled it out again, it had become a great pot brimming over with grain. When Udero Lal was ten and old enough to be invested with the sacred thread, he asked to be given a guru. He took his father and mother to the river bank and found sitting near it the great God Shiva. Udero Lal went up fearlessly to the mighty God and told him that he had come in search of a guru. The god replied "Why do you, who are the guru of gurus, want a guru?" Udero Lal pleaded that even Vishnu's avatars, such as Rama and Krishna had had their gurus, why then should one be denied to him? It so chanced that the saint Gorakhnath passed by at that moment and Shiva bade him take Udero Lal as his pupil. Gorakhnath did so and taught him all his holiness and wisdom.

Now Udero Lal had a cousin called Phugar, who was greatly attached to him. He made Phugar his disciple and taught him the learning which he had received from Gorakhnath. One day to test Phugar's faith he told him that he wished to be alone and meditate. But Phugar refused to leave his master's side. "Will you plunge with me into the Indus?" asked Udero Lal. "Where you go, I go," was the reply. Udero Lal took his cousin's hand and dived into the river. A few minutes later they came to the surface and found themselves in mid-stream between Rohri and Sukkur. In front of them was a little island on which they climbed. This was the famous island of Zinda Pir, of whom more hereafter. Master and pupil stayed there some weeks until Udero Lal learnt that Ratno and Devki were both very ill at Nasarpur. He reached his birthplace in time to bid them farewell. But their deaths preyed on his mind and he longed to rejoin the mighty river from which he had sprung. He first called to him his elder brothers Somo and Bhayandev and bade them give up the things of this world and like Phugar become his disciples. But though they promised always to worship light and water, they would not give up all and follow him. Udero Lal then declared that Phugar would be his only disciple. He called him and gave him the following seven gifts:—

A Var or ring that fulfilled every wish of the wearer.

A Jot or lamp that gave to him who looked into its flame a vision of the Most High.

A Kanta or quilt that guarded the wearer from demons and from human weapons.

A Deg or cooking pot that remained always full of food.

A Tegh or sword that put to flight the five evil passions—kam or lust, krodh or anger, lobh or greed, moh or love of the things of this world and ahankar or selfishness.

A Jhari or pitcher that remained always full of Ganges water.

A Daklo or musical instrument that reproduced the songs sung in heaven.

When twelve years old Udero Lal bade Phugar choose a spot, whereon to build him a temple, as he meant soon to leave the earth. Phugar chose an open field owned by a Memon. The saint asked the Memon to give him the land. The Memon refused but offered to sell it. Udero Lal scratched with his spear the surface of the earth and shewed the astonished Memon treasures of gold and silver. Then he drove his spear deep into the ground and it became a mighty kabar tree. The Memon was so startled that he went away to take counsel of his wife. On his return he bade the saint take the field as a gift. All he asked, was that he might be the majavar or attendant of Udero Lal's tomb. The saint blessed him and promised him that his life long he would never lack food. Udero Lal took another spear and smote the ground with it. Up spouted a fountain of clear water. He mounted his horse; the earth opened in front of him. Spurring his horse he leapt into the yawning pit.

At first Phugar was broken-hearted and nearly died of grief. One night he saw in a dream Udero Lal who bade him put away his grief and build a temple on the spot where the saint had vanished. Where the water had spouted from the ground he was to sink a well and near it to build a rest-house. When the saint's wishes were known, all Nasarpur flocked to Phugar's aid. Even the wicked Marak and his minister and kazi offered their help. But while the Hindus wished to build a temple, Marak and the Musalmans wished to build a mosque and quarrels broke out between them. At last they resolved to take the advice of Udero Lal himself. All one night they kept vigil until they heard a voice that said " In my sight there is neither caste nor creed." Pacified, they built both mosque and temple. Of the temple Phugar was made guardian and Marak named the Memon the mujavar of the mosque. From that day on, lamps have burnt night and day in both temple and mosque. The rest-house built by Phugar may be seen to this day and near it is the well, which grateful pilgrims have called Balambho or the well of ever-running water.

JINDA PIR.

In my last chapter I related how the saint Udero Lal and his disciple Phugar, after diving into the Indus near Nasarpur, came to the surface between Rohri and Sukkur and landed on a rocky island. The island is still there and bears on its rounded back a temple to Zinda Pir. According to the Hindus Zinda or the living Pir is none other than Udero Lal. According to the Musulmans he is somebody quite different.

According to the Musulmans, the river Indus flowed once past Alor and not past Rohri. Somewhere in the tenth century A. D. a Hindu king called Dalurai ruled at Alor. He and his brother Sasu Rai practised every kind of abomination. Such were their wickedness and their vigour that they enforced the *jus primae noctis* on every young lady, who was married within their dominions. On one occasion a pious Musulman merchant named Shah Hussein was going down the Indus, so that he might sail from its mouth to Arabia and visit Mecca. With him journeyed his beautiful daughter. On the way they stopped at Alor and the beauty of the merchant's daughter was noised abroad and reached the ears of king Dalurai, who instantly demanded that she should be sent to his palace. But neither Shah Hussain nor his daughter had any wish that she should become the concubine of a Hindu king. They both prayed fervently to Zinda Pir. He appeared in a vision to the young girl and bade her and her father board their boat and weigh anchor. They did so and the stream at Zinda Pir's command, changed its course and leaving Alor, brought the boat and its burden to Rohri. When Shah Hussain awoke next morning, he was close to Udero Lal's island. To it he moored his boat and built the temple, that stands there to this day. On it are the words "Darga Ali." These give the date 341 A. H. or 961 A. D.

The above tale explains the foundation of the temple but it does not tell us who the saint himself was. Earnest Christians will hear with surprise that he is none other than their old friend the prophet Elijah. They will probably exclaim with Moliere's M. Géronte "Mais que diable allait-il faire dans cette galère ?" It was this way. According to the Islamic legend, Elijah was in a former life a very holy man indeed, named Balya Ebn Malkan. Because of the colour of his garment, he was also known as Al Khisr or the Prophet of the Green robe. Balya Ebn Malkan was the contemporary of Moses and in Chapter 18 of the Koran we find him going with Moses on a most interesting circular tour. The story is shortly this. Once the great Jewish sage was preaching to his people with such wisdom and eloquence that at the close of his sermon, they asked him whether there was any man in the world wiser than he was. Conscious of his great powers, he replied in the negative. That night God appeared to him in a dream, rebuked him for his vanity and told him that his servant Al Khisr was wiser than he was. Moses asked where he could meet this paragon of wisdom. God answered that Moses would find Al Khisr near a rock where two seas met. If Moses took a fish with him in a basket, the spot where he missed the fish would be the place where the prophet of the green robe dwelt. Moses took Joshua and a fish with him and in due course missed the fish and found the prophet. Moses asked leave to be Al Khisr's disciple and to learn his wisdom. Al Khisr answered that if Moses came and suffered all that Al Khisr did without asking any questions he could be his disciple, but not otherwise. Moses promised to do so and the two prophets went to the sea shore and boarded a ship. Al Khisr at once made a hole in the bottom of it. Moses indignantly asked whether he wanted to drown every soul on board. But his companion sternly reminded Moses of his promise and left the ship. A little later they met a youth. Al Khisr struck him so violently on the head that he died at once. Moses angrily asked why he had taken an innocent life. Al Khisr again rebuked him and went his way to a city. There they saw a crumbling wall which the citizens could not repair. Al Khisr touched the wall with his hand and it became as if it had been newly built. Moses asked him why he did not claim from the citizens a rich reward. Al Khisr then turned on his unfortunate disciple and cast him forth. "Three times" said Al Khisr, "you have broken your promise and questioned my acts. You are not worthy to be my pupil. I made a hole in the ship to save it from the king's men. Had it been seaworthy, they would have taken the ship by force and given the owner nothing. I killed the youth, because although the son of true believers, he was himself an unbeliever and I feared lest he should corrupt the faith of his parents. I repaired the wall for nothing, because hidden under it was a treasure, which a righteous man had buried there before he died. He left two orphan sons and it is God's will that when they reach man's state, they shall find their father's treasure."

During Al Khisr's existence as Balya Ebn Malkan he found and drank the waters of immortality. That was why as Elijah he did not die, but was transported to heaven in a fiery chariot. And because he drank the waters of immortality, he is always connected with running water; and with what nobler stream could he be associated than the Indus, as it passes through the Sukkur gorge?

To-day the special duty of Zinda Pir is to help the Indus boatmen when in distress. His functions are thus similar to those of the ancient Dioscuri, of whom Macaulay wrote:

"Safe comes the ship to harbour
Through billows and through gales
If once the great twin brethren
Sit shining on the sails."

The Indus is terribly dangerous in July and August, when the mighty river swollen by the melting snows of the Himalayas comes tearing and tossing through the gorge. So one who has seen the Indus in flood can ever forget the sight. It is then that the boatmen pray to Al Khisr. To attend more closely to their prayers, Al Khisr comes in person to his temple and for forty days sits in a little niche specially reserved for him. The niche has comfortable cushions and in front of it is laid a copy of the Koran. The saint is invisible, but the mujavars or attendants of the mosque or temple know that he has been there; for when the forty days begin they place in front of the niche the Koran open at the first page and when the forty days are past, they find the Koran open at the last page. Elijah has in his leisure moments read the Koran from cover to cover.

ABDUL LATIF, THE AUTHOR OF SHAH JO RISALO.

Abdul Latif's grandfather Shah Karim was a Sayad of Matari and so celebrated for his piety that his mausoleum at Bulree in the Karachi District is still the scene of an annual fair. Shah Karim was born in 1558 A. D. and died it is said in 1660 A. D. The tale runs that while Shah Karim was yet a boy, he met a fakir in a mosque. The fakir had been a soldier, but the awful consequences of war had so preyed on his mind that he had deserted the army. Shah Karim became the spiritual follower of this fakir and grew up so renowned a saint that it was commonly said that whereas Bahawaldin, a rival saint, could make a live man dead, Shah Karim could make a dead man alive. Shah Karim removed to Bulree and had three sons, one of whom Shah Habib was the father of Abdul Latif, the subject of our article. The date of his birth is to be found in the Persian line on his mausoleum.

Gardeed mahw ishk wujoode Latif Meer.

(The spirit of the lordly Latit was absorbed in love).

According to the Abjad system, this gives the date of his death as 1751 A. D. As he was sixty-three when he died, he was born in 1688 A. D. He thus lived to see the establishment of the Kalhora dynasty, the invasion of Nadir Shah in 1739 and that of Ahmad Shah Durani in 1748.

Abdul Latif fell in love with a beautiful Moghul girl, the daughter of one Mirza Beg. He was said to be a descendant of Mirza Jani Beg of the Turkhan dynasty, whose tombs are among the Makli Hills. Abdul Latif serenaded the lovely girl in verses written by himself, until he was ordered off the premises by her father. Undefeated, he turned himself into a pigeon and cooed his love to the fair maiden from the trellis of her balcony. Even so Mirza Beg with a father's vigilance pierced his disguise and threatened to set his falcons on Abdul Latif, unless he flew away. The unhappy Abdul Latif went and sat on a sandhill and watched the house of the Moghul girl with such devotion from afar, that the sandhill grew round him until it had covered all but his head. A goatherd Jam by name who passed saw his head sticking out. He told Abdul Latif's father, Shah Habib, who had his son dug up. But Abdul Latif was still beside himself with amorous passion. He went to a carpenter and induced him to hollow out a tamarisk tree, that stood by itself in a cemetery. Latif got inside the hollow tree and looked out on the world through a single cleft. In vain Shah Habib sought everywhere for his son. At last his lamentations touched the heart of the carpenter, who shewed him his son's hiding place. Shah Habib took his son home, but an evil fate overtook the carpenter. As a punishment for betraying Abdul Latif's hiding place, he became a leper. Shah Habib licked the sores, so that they healed, all save one obstinate one that remained open on his forehead.

Abdul Latif did not stay long in his father's house, but began to wander about Sind. One day he came to Lakhpat. There he saw some Sami fakirs worshipping an idol, probably of Parvati. They were pouring milk over it and as they did so, they repeated "O Grandmother, drink this milk." But the idol being of stone, hearkened not at all. Latif went into the village, bought a bowl full of milk and stood close to the idol. In one hand he held his shoe and then he said to the idol "O Grandmother of the Samis, drink this milk or I shall beat you with this shoe." The idol no longer hearkened not. Terrified at the threat, it drank up all the milk in the bowl. The Sami fakirs were filled with wonder and envy. After Abdul Latif had left the spot, they plotted to kill and eat him, so as to obtain his supernatural powers. They invited him to a feast, intending to make their guest the principal dish. But Abdul Latif by his inner knowledge guessed their wickedness and departed.

As he journeyed he met another fakir, whose beautiful face was haggard and worn, as if with care. As the fakir walked, he cried always " Jhal fakir, Hal fakir (Take it fakir, go fakir). Abdul Latif asked him why he did it. The fakir refused to tell him, unless Abdul Latif promised to help him to win what he sought. " If," said the fakir, " I win my goal through your help, I shall get you a Burat or letter of salvation." The saint gave his promise and the fakir told him what ailed him. Some months before he had met a jungle tribe and had daily begged from them. Whenever he did so, a lovely maiden of the tribe had given him alms and as she gave them, she repeated these words " Jhal fakir, Hal fakir." The beauty of the girl's voice and face had burnt into his brain. When the tribe left, he could think of nothing but of her and he set out to seek her. As he went, he repeated her words in the hope of finding her. Abdul Latif by his inner knowledge soon located the jungle tribe. With the fakir he went to their camp and began to recite to them his verses. They were so charmed with the verses that they asked him to name his reward. He told them to send the lovely girl to the hut wherein he had put his humble belongings. The girl was sent and in the hut the fakir awaited her. Their eyes met, but the storm of passion that swept over both of them was too mighty for their strength to bear. They fell back lifeless into Abdul Latif's arms. He called the girl's parents and told them the tale of the fakir's wooing and its tragic end. At his request the man and the maiden were buried in the same grave, That night Abdul Latif watched by the grave, for he had not yet received the Burat or letter of salvation. At midnight a woman's hand rose from the grave and offered him a letter. But Abdul Latif doubted the virtue of a Burat that came from a woman. " I shall not take the Burat," he said, " unless he who promised it to me gives it." The girl's voice answered that that was impossible. The fakir for very shame, she said, dared ask nothing from God. He had not been able to hide his love but to the whole world had told his sorrows. Her love had been as ardent as his, but she had had the strength to hide it. It was at her request that God had given the Burat and the saint must take it from her hands.

Another time Abdul Latif went to Kotri and there exposed the impostures of the Mullas who surrounded the governor Lalla Beg. At their instigation the cruel ruler ordered Abdul Latif to be impaled and then cut to pieces. When the executioners went to Shah Latif's house to seize him, they found him already dead and dismembered. As they returned to tell Lalla Beg, they saw the saint standing in the roadside alive and well. They spoke of these marvels to Lalla Beg, who at once remitted the sentence.

Abdul Latif, before he started on his wanderings, had, because of his unsatisfied love for the Moghul girl, cursed the whole tribe of the Moghuls, who then lived in Sind. All this time his curse had been quietly working. One by one they had died off, including the hard hearted Mirza Beg. Of all the Moghul children only one boy Gulla by name survived and the beautiful girl, whom Abdul Latif loved. Freed from her father's cruelty by his death, she no longer hesitated but sought out and found her lover. With her she took her kinsman Gulla. Abdul Latif overjoyed at her coming recalled his curse and Gulla lived to be the ancestor of many Moghuls thereafter.

Abdul Latif, or as we should now call him Latif Shah, did not settle down to enjoy his wedded happiness at Varsum, where Shah Habib had lived and where he himself had been born. Near it was the tomb of an earlier saint Nuh Halani. The jealous spirit of the dead saint envied Latif Shah's happiness and glory. Nuh Halani's spirit haunted Shah Latif night and day. In despair Shah Latif sought the aid of Bahawal Hak, a holy man of Multan. He advised him to consult Sayad Mahmad Massum Shah. The latter in turn advised him to migrate to Bhitta, then a desolate mound of sand. Latif Shah obeyed the Sayad, but even at Bhitta—*tantaene animis caelestibus irae* —he was not safe from persecution. Nuh Halani changed the spirit of a former disciple into a huge snake and bade it bite the unhappy Shah Latif. But the latter prayed to Sayad Mahmad Massum Shah and with his aid and his own sanctity, he tamed the snake and kept it in a cage, as a trophy of his victory. Nuh Halani's descendant Makhdum Mahmad Zaman could not bear the sight. He redeemed the snake at the cost of a vast stretch of country and turning the snake again into a spirit, sent it back to do service to Nuh Halani in the house of Hades.

"Happy is the wooing that's not long in the doing," is an old English proverb and perhaps it was of the long delay in the union of Shah Latif and his bride,that they were not blessed with children. Two legends are told to account for this calamity. One is that Shah Latif drew after him the son of one Jani, who in anger cursed the saint that his wife should bear him no sons. Latif Shah accepted the curse and consoled himself with the remark that his disciples were his sons. The second legend is that Latif Shah's wife, a year after marriage, was expecting a child. After the manner of women in delicate health, she had strange longings. One day she sent her maidservant to a great distance to get a certain kind of fish. Latif

Shah missed the maid-servant and asked whither she had gone. On learning what had happened, he flew into a rage—if I may say such a thing of so holy a man. He cursed his unborn child, saying " If the child gives all this trouble now, what terrible trouble it will give when it is grown up ! May such a blossom be nipped in the bud." The child was still-born and no other came to soothe the poor mother's grief.

It was at Bhitta that Shah Latif wrote the Shah jo Rasalo. When he had finished it, his two faithful disciples Tamar and Hashim brought it to him. As he read over the lines in which he had told the sorrows of Saswi, he exclaimed that the verses did not truly convey a spiritual meaning, but were full of sinful passion. As he said this, he flung the great work into the Kirar Dandh, a lake close by. His horrified disciples beseeched him to let them write the Shah jo Rasalo from memory. Reluctantly he consented and the Shah jo Rasalo was saved.

Shah Latif died in 1751 at the age of 63, three years after Ahmad Shah Durani's invasion. The saint's body lies in a splendid tomb designed by a celebrated mason of Sukkur, under the orders of Ghulam Shah Kalhoro. The door with silver bars was added by Mir Mahmad and a deep well for the use of pilgrims was sunk in the courtyard by one Laung Fakir. The Pir of the tomb is the descendant of Jam the goatherd, who found Shah Latif buried up to the neck in sand. Every Friday night pilgrims keep watch by the tomb and sing passages from the saint's immortal poem. This custom had its origin in a dream dreamt by his disciple Hashim. After his master's death, he was ill of fever and could not get well. One night Shah Latif appeared to him in a vision and bade him recite on the following Friday some lines from the Shah jo Rasalo. He did so and was cured.

MAKDUM NIAMAT ULLAH AND MAKDUM NUH.

Early in the 18th century the greatest saint in Sind was Makdum Niamat Ullah, the father of a still greater religious luminary, the famous Makdum Nuh. So renowned was Makdum Niamat Ullah that an ancient fakir more than a hundred years old and known as La Ikhtyar or the Independent One was so affected by the stories told of the saintly Makdum Niamat Ullah, that he gave up his independent life and went to Torio in the Hala taluka on the chance of seeing the object of his admiration. Torio was not Makdum Niamat's usual place of residence, but La Ikhtyar had had a vision that it would be at Torio that he would see the Desired One.

After some weeks Makdum Niamat Ullah did go to Torio on business and passed La Ikhtyar, as he sat on his cot. At once the old fakir recognised the passer-by from the radiant glow on his countenance. The fakir got off his cot and made the saint sit on it and knelt at his feet. But as Makdum sat, the fakir's tame birds of which he had a large number suddenly flew away. The saint asked the reason and was told that he would be the father of a son who would love to shoot birds. When the fakir's pets learnt this, they had flown away in terror. After bidding the fakir goodbye, Makdum Niamat Ullah walked into the bazaar. As he passed a Hindu's shop, the owner's wife fell so desperately in love with him, that she begged him to take her away from her husband and marry her. The saint could not stoop to such wickedness ; but to get rid of her importunities, he promised to fetch her away that very night. He left her and went to take a siesta in the shade of a high wall, some streets away. As he slept, a certain Amin, the chief of the Lankas, passed by on his way to Lower Sind. He had with him a comely marriageable daughter, who at once fell in love with the sleeping saint. Amin woke up Makdum Niamat Ullah and offered his daughter to him in marriage. The saint gladly accepted the offer and was married to the beautiful girl the same evening. Next morning the Hindu woman saw the saint and going up to him, reproached him for not keeping his tryst. The saint explained that he was now a married man and must cleave to his wife. He, however, blessed the amorous Hindu lady and nine months from that very day, she presented to her husband a son called Zabhar.

On the same day as Zabhar was born, the wife of Makhdum Niamat Ullah presented her lord with a son, the celebrated Makdum Nuh. Even as a tiny baby, Makdum Nuh shewed his precocious saintliness. When only six days old, he compelled the fakir La Ikhtyar, who was his devoted slave, to go through the ceremony of becoming his disciple. The fakir lived until his infantile preceptor was five years old; then he died at the ripe age of 106 and his tomb may still be seen at Old Hala. His reputation for independence has survived him and many persons who are in difficulties still visit his tomb and ask the Independent One for his advice.

Makdum Nuh took to the Koran, as the proverbial duck takes to water. At the age of seven he knew the mighty book by heart. At the age of fourteen he was vouchsafed a vision of no less a personage than Mahomed himself. As Makdum Nuh was washing in the river his slate on which he had written some lines of the Koran, he saw a boat approach. In it were the Prophet, his son-in-law Ali and Huzrat Isa or Jesus. The boat stopped and the Holy Prophet called Makdum Nuh by name. The boy went up to the boat and Jesus took his slate and wrote on one side of it fourteen lines. Then Ali took it and wrote on it eighteen lines and the boat glided away. The astonished Makdum Nuh took his slate to his teacher, who found that what was written on it far transcended even his understanding. He asked his pupil what hand had written the lines. Makdum Nuh told him about the three strangers in the boat; thereupon his teacher guessed what had happened and embraced the boy, as one to whom the Prophet had vouchsafed a vision.

Makdum Nuh became when he grew up, as prophesied by the fakir, a great bird-shot; but he also worked many and mighty miracles. His most famous achievement was connected with the great mosque at Tatta. This mosque had been built at a cost of many lakhs of rupees by the orders of the Moghul Emperor. When it was completed, the faithful noted with dismay that it did not correctly face the Kaaba. This was too dreadful for words; for unless a mosque faces the Kaaba properly, it is useless. The faithful, too, of Tatta had been bragging loudly to their neighbours about their future mosque and they now would be exposed to their mocking laughter. The faithful of Tatta appealed to Makdum Nuh. He called to his aid another holy man Ali Shirazi and they assailed Allah with continuous and soul-compelling prayers. At first nothing happened and the faithful began to murmur discordantly at the failure of the two saints. "But verily" as the Koran has it, "some suspicions are as sins." Another half hour's steady prayer and the great edifice began to quiver. Makdum Nuh then called on all true Musulmans present to tie ropes to the building and pull it round; and lo! and behold! under the combined pressure of the prayers of the saints and the pushings of the faithful, the great mosque turned round slowly and then stopped dead. It had come to face exactly in the true direction of Mecca.

Even a man so holy as Makdum Nuh could not escape from the malice of mankind. He had two great friends Muzaffar and Salar. Salar had promised his daughter in marriage to

Muzaffar's son. Unhappily a quarrel broke out between these two eminent men and Salar refused to give his daughter. Now in Sind marriageable girls are few and this was a home thrust. Muzaffar complained to Makdum Nuh, who after hearing both sides ordered Salar to keep his promise. Salar obeyed, *la mort dans lâme;* but he vented his spleen by cursing the said saint in the following quatrain:

> " O Makhdum, you have done an act not pleasing to God; You have set at nought what God had ordained.
>
> You will suffer by having your corpse put in three different places after your death."

The curse of this impious blasphemer was unhappily fulfilled. The river Indus twice threatened the spot where Makdum Nuh had been buried. The second time the river approached so rapidly that the disciples had to remove their master's body in broad daylight instead of at night, as was seemly. Heaven, however, came to their help. As they began to lift the body from the grave, the sky became overcast and a mist as thick as a London fog spread over the land, so that none could see the decaying remains of one who in life had been strong and beautiful. The saint's body found its last resting place about two miles to the west of Old Hala. A small town has sprung up round the tomb and is known as Murtazabad. A beautiful mausoleum now stands over Makdum Nuh's grave and the cupola over it was erected in 1795 A. D. by Mir Fateh Ali Khan Talpur. On the tomb were engraved the following words in order to silence possible slanderers of the dead man:

> " If the wind were to blow furiously all over the world
> It could never extinguish the lamp of those accepted by the Most High,

Men who spit on a lamp, lit by Almighty God soon find that they have in their folly, set fire to their own beards."

According to my chronicler, these lines had an excellent effect. They were the proper stuff to hand out to the back-biters.

HAIDARABAD.

Haidarabad was once known as Nerankot and the king of it was Raja Neran. He had a beautiful daughter, who, from the exquisite skill with which she darkened her eyes with Kanjal or lampblack, reddened her cheeks with rouge and coloured her finger nails with henna, was known as Nigar or the Painted lady. Her courage was, if possible, greater even than her beauty. She scorned to ride camels or horses, as other well born Hindu ladies did. The only beast she would bestride was a lion and every evening outside Nerankot she might have been seen riding a splendid maned lion, who, when bridled by her, was as docile as the meekest ambling palfrey, to the touch of her finger on the reins. Nor would she suffer cowardice in others. She vowed and made public her vow that she would wed no man who feared to saddle and mount a lion.

It so happened that Shah Makai and Haidar Ali came about this time to Sind. Shah Makai's real name was Shah Mahmud ; but because he lived at Maka or Mecca, he was known as Shah Makai. Haidar Ali's real name was Ali. But, because as a child he had torn to pieces a live snake with his bare hands, he was called Haidar Ali or the Ali who tore the "Hai" or snake. His fortune was as great as his childhood foretold ; for in due course he became the son-in-law of the holy prophet and the fourth Imam of the Faithful. As the two friends journeyed through Sind, they came to hear the fame of Nigar's beauty and courage. Straightway they hastened to Nerankot and one evening Shah Makai saw the lovely girl astride of her lion, riding outside the walls. He fell madly in love with her. Then he heard that she had vowed not to marry anyone, unless he could tame and mount a lion. Shah Makai as a true and devout believer, had but little difficulty in performing this feat and the next time that Nigar rode abroad, she saw to her surprise and pleasure Shah Makai astride of a maned lion, hardly less majestic than her own. She asked him who he was; and learning that he had broken in the lion for love of her, she vowed that she would wed him and no other. Shah Makai sought an audience of Neran Raja and asked for his daughter's hand. Nigar, too, pressed her father to give his consent to the marriage. But the proud King's heart was as hard as stone and although he heard the full tale of Shah Makai's courtship, he refused to give his daughter to one who was not a Hindu, but a Mleccha. With contumely he drove Shah Makai from his Court. When Nigar vowed that in spite of her father she would wed the bold Arabian, Raja Neran threw her into a well and had a huge stone put over its mouth. The evil news reached Shah Makai. He tried to move the stone; but it was so big, that even he, saint though he was, failed. He implored the help of Haidar 'Ali. To that pillar of Islam the task was light. He mounted his white mule Dhul Dhul and made it dance on the top of the stone. Then he dismounted and throwing himself at full length on the ground, he prayed Allah to remove it. He had hardly finished his prayer, when the stone rolled aside and Nigar with Haidar Ali's help was able to climb out of the well. He gave her to Shah Makai, who carried her off in triumph. But Haidar Ali cursed the wicked Neran; and stretching wide the five fingers of his right hand made the *bhundo* sign at him.

Not long afterwards the curse was fulfilled. The Arabs landing on the sea coast of Sind swept through the land, stormed Nerankot and killed Raja Neran. For many centuries Nerankot lay in ruins. Then the wise and pious Ghulam Shah Kalhoro came to the spot and deeming it well fitted for the site of his capital city, he rebuilt Nerankot. While the new fortress was building, he raised a small mud stronghold close to the spot where Shah Makai and the beautiful Painted Lady were in their old age buried side by side. When Nerankot was finished, Ghulam Shah Kalhoro went to live in it and renamed it Haidarabad after Haidar Ali. He gave his mud stronghold to the Fakirs who guarded Shah Makai's tomb. Upto Burton's time a lion—said to be a descendant of Nigar's riding lion—used to be kept in a cage under a tamarind tree, close to Shah Makai's last resting place. The tree still stands, but the lion has vanished. The rise in the price of lion's food was no doubt the cause of its disappearance.

About a quarter of a mile from the tomb of Shah Makai is another small but holy building known as Shah Kadam. Within it are preserved the stones on which Haidar Ali's white mule Dhul Dhul did its miracle-working dance. Its hoof marks may still be seen stamped deep in the stone. By its side a slab bears the marks of Haidar Ali's hands, knees, feet and forehead, which he made when he prostrated himself in prayer before Allah. And a third stone bears the marks of the saint's fingers and thumb when he made the *bhundo* at Raja Neran. So violent was the Imam's curse that it has lived on, *monumentum aere perennius.* The well into which Nigar was thrown is one of the three inside Nerankot, but none could tell me with certainty which it was. Perhaps the most interesting relic of that golden time is a great "djar" tree that grows near Shah Makai's tomb. The guardian of the shrine assured me that it had grown from a bit of stick, which the saint had one day used as a toothbrush and then carelessly thrown aside.

BRAHMANABAD.—I.

The ruined town of Brahmanabad, probably the most interesting spot in Sind, lies about eleven miles from Shahdadpur. A road sufficiently good for a Ford Car leads thither and a run there on a cold weather morning is a bracing and exhilarating experience. When Brahmanabad is reached one sees, as far as the eye can range, an endless waste of brick ruins, the site of a once mighty city. It flourished in the time of Alexander. It was still great in the eighth century when Mahomed Kasim invaded Sind. What caused its downfall? The whole question was admirably discussed in 1854 by Mr. Bellasis of the Indian Civil Service. His conclusion was that the city had been overwhelmed by an earthquake, which at the same time changed the bed of the Indus, formerly close by the city walls and the source of its greatness. The destruction of Brahmanabad, wrote Mr. Bellasis, was so complete that it could not have been caused by a fire or by a hostile force. There were, moreover, no signs of fire. There were quantities of jewellery among the ruins, which neither fugitive inhabitants nor an enemy would have left. At the same time there were many skeletons visible in corners and doorways—the skeletons of men and women overwhelmed, no doubt, as they sought to escape. The skeletons have long ago gone to manure the neighbouring fields, just as the bricks of the houses in which they once lived are to be found in the villages round about. Still we may safely accept the evidence of Mr Bellasis as well as the accuracy of his conclusions. But if Brahmanabad was overwhelmed by an earthquake, what were the circumtsances attending it? We have no historical record

But there exist two legends—a Musulman and a Hindu legend. They differ widely from each other, only agreeing in this that the end of Brahmanabad came because of God's wrath at the wickedness of its ruler, Dalu Rai. I shall relate the Musulman legend first. It is to be found in the Tufat-ul-Kiram and runs somewhat as follows:

Once upon a time there ruled over the city of Brahmanabad a Hindu king, called Dalu Rai (May Allah confound him!) whose wickedness is still well remembered in the land of Sind. He had, however, a brother called Chota Amrani, who had given up *kufar* or ingratitude and had won immortal happiness by embracing Islam. He had left Brahmanabad and had committed to memory the whole Koran and also all the customs of the True Believers. On his return to the city his relatives wanted him to marry; but king Dalu Rai said with a cruel sneer "He is a renegade. Let him go on a pilgrimage to Mecca and there wed the daughter of some famous Arab; but he shall not marry the daughter of any Hindu subject of mine!"

Chota Amrani feared to stay longer in Brahmanabad, so he set out on a pilgrimage to Mecca. After many hardships and dangers he reached the Holy City. As he walked through the streets, he passed a shop, wherein a woman, instead of attending to her customers was reading aloud the Koran. Chota Amrani stopped to listen. The woman saw him and asked him why he did not pass on. "I have stopped," said Chota Amrani, "to listen to the words of Holy Writ. I have learnt the Koran by heart; but if you will teach me its various readings, I shall become your slave." "Nay," said the woman, "I am not fit to teach you. I have a teacher of my own. She is a maiden and you cannot enter her home in a man's dress. But if you change your clothes and dress like a girl, I shall take you to her." Chota Amrani who was still quite young and without any beard on his chin, agreed. He dressed up as a girl and was taken to the house of the learned maiden by the woman in the shop. The maiden's name was Fatima and she readily undertook the instruction of the foreign girl, who had come from so far off to see Mecca. One day the shopwoman asked Fatima some questions concerning the marriage of her daughter. Fatima, who was skilled in astrology as well as in matters religious, answered the questions with ease. Chota Amrani then to test the maiden said " As you can tell the future of others, you can surely tell your own future." Fatima replied " My fate is to be married to a man from Sind." " But when ? " asked the astonished visitor. " In no long time," replied Fatima. " But where is the man ? " asked Chota Amrani. Fatima pretended to consult her astrological books and said with a smile " You are the man." Then she added " Begone and come no longer in the garb of a girl. Put on a man's dress and ask formally for my hand, for I am destined to be yours."

Chota Amrani, abashed at the penetration of his disguise, went away and returned dressed as a man. He formally asked for the hand of Fatima. His request was granted and she became his wife.

After two or three months had passed, Chota Amrani told Fatima that he must take her back with him to Sind. Fatima made no objection and they set sail for the land of the Indus river. When they reached Brahmanabad, they found that Dalu Rai had recently issued a law that every young married woman should be brought to his couch for at least one night. He therefore demanded that Chota Amrani should send Fatima to his palace. Chota Amrani refused and Dalu Rai did nothing for the moment. But one day when Chota Amrani was absent from the city, Dalu Rai forced his way into his brother's house and tried to seduce Fatima. The noble lady virtuously resisted all his efforts to lead her astray and fortunately before he could use violence to her, Chota Amrani returned. He drove the wicked king from his house and instantly left Brahmanabad with Fatima. As he left, a voice from heaven was heard to say " This city will soon be swallowed because of its king's wickedness. Let those who are warned flee from the accursed spot or keep watch against the day of atonement." A few obeyed and shook from their feet the dust of the doomed city, but most of the people paid no heed. The first night the city was spared, because an old woman working at a wheel kept awake all night, as the voice had commanded. The second night an oil presser kept watch unceasingly. But the third night the inhabitants forgot the divine warning. Suddenly, while all slept the entire city was swallowed up. Of all its splendid buildings only one minaret remained, as an example and a warning to other kings and peoples.

BRAHMANABAD.—II.

Now let us turn to the Hindu legend which I came across in a Sind magazine. It ran as follows :—

Once upon a time Brahmanabad, now a heap of ruins, was the glory of all Sind. It stood on an oasis in the desert ; and to guard its people from sudden raids by desert tribes, one of its kings had built round it a great wall. Beneath the wall flowed the river Indus, on whose waters the merchant ships of Brahmanabad carried the city's commerce up and down Sind. Inside the walls were rich houses, countless gardens, and a mighty tower, that served as a landmark for miles around. About a mile and a half from Brahmanabad was the royal suburb of Dalor in which stood the king's palace and the quarters of his guards. Some five miles from Brahmanabad stood the suburb of Depur. Therein lived the ministers with their public offices and their record-rooms and storehouses. Along the banks of the river was a collection of huts, wherein lived a wild gipsy tribe known as Madu. They lived by selling milk and ghi to the rich burghers of Brahmanabad.

The reigning king Amrai was beloved by his people and when his queen died, he would not give her place to another. He devoted his life to the upbringing of their only son, prince Dalu Rai. Unhappily so evil was the lad's nature, that the more care the king spent on him the worse he grew. He gathered round him a band of bad companions and all day and every day the royal palace resounded with the cries of the prince's victims. At last the king out of all patience, shut up his son in the tall tower which looked over the country round Brahmanabad. But the fickle mob at once turned round " What a cruel father ! " they cried. " Fancy treating thus the heir to the throne ! " King Amrai consulted his ministers and they advised him to free his son, but at the same time to put in charge of him some wise and virtuous old man, who by example and precept would show him the error of his ways. King Amrai thought their advice good and freeing the prince, appointed a wise old man to look after him and to teach him. Although the king said nothing to Dalu Rai, the latter guessed, when an aged pandit called on him, that he was in some way to be over him. He instantly resolved to treat the old man in such a way that neither he nor any other old man in the kingdom would accept the post again. He pretended to listen with the greatest attention to all the old man's words and seemed so eager to do what was right, that the sage thought the prince the most charming of pupils. After some hours of talk, the prince made his master dine with him. During the meal the old man talked as one inspired ; and as he talked, the prince's servants filled his glass over and over again with drugged wine. Before the meal was over the poor old pandit was fast asleep. The prince had him put to bed and as he lay asleep, the prince's barber shaved off the sage's moustaches and stuck in their place crow's feathers. Next morning when the old man awoke, he passed his hand over his face and found the horrible thing that had been done to him. He rose, fled from the prince's house and threw himself at king Amrai's feet and told him of the prince's cruel trick. The king soothed the old man as best he could ; but he was so affected, that he never shewed himself in the Darbar Hall again.

The prince was thus free to act as he pleased. One evening he and his good for nothing companions went out a hawking. Game was scarce and their hawks caught nothing. At last they reached a well near a Madu hamlet not far from the town. Vexed at their ill luck, they loosed their hawks at some tame pigeons that belonged to the villagers and happened to be circling near the well. All the pigeons but one took shelter in their dovecotes. One pigeon flew into the air followed by the prince's hawk. For some time the two birds soared in the air, one unable to rise above the other. At last the hawk's strong wings bore it above the pigeon and it made its swoop. The frightened pigeon dropped like a stone to the ground at the feet of a Madu maiden of 16, who was filling her jar at the well. The girl picked up the pigeon and stroking its feathers put it in her bosom. The hawk robbed of its prey, flew back to perch on the wrist of the prince's huntsman. The prince rode up to the girl and with an evil smile on his lips, told her that she might keep the pigeon, He would not hunt it now that it had taken shelter in her bosom. The girl turned on him scornfully and said " A fine hunter you are to hawk a tame pigeon!" The prince pretended to be sorry for what he had done and then asked the girl to give him a drink of water from his jar. But the Madu maiden disliking his looks and tone, told him to get one of his servants to fetch water for him. But the prince pressed her, pleading that their horses were restive. Reluctantly the girl went close to him to give him a cup of water. Suddenly he caught her by the waist and swung her in front of him. A moment later he and his companions were riding as fast as they could to the prince's palace. Some Madu men ran after them but in vain. The prince carried off the girl and the men with him said in jest " The prince's hawk lost its prey, but the prince had better luck!" As the party neared the palace, they passed an aged Brahman, who, hearing the cries of the struggling girl, begged the prince to free her. But Dalu Rai only snarled at him to mind his own business. The Brahman, who was a mighty anchorite, flew into a passion and cursed him. " As a punishment for your cruelty," he cried, " you will never live to be old. Your city will be destroyed and you will perish with it so suddenly, that you will not have time to give even a handful of grain in charity!"

The prince paid little heed to the anchorite's curse, but bore his prey inside the palace. There he found everyone excited as the princess had just borne her lord a son. But the prince pushed past his servants and took the Madu girl to a distant part of the palace and there tried to win her consent. But she scornfully rejected his promises of rich clothes and fine jewels. At last when he had lost all patience and was about to offer her violence, he heard a knock at his door. It was a messenger who brought the news that king Amrai was dead.

At the same time he told the prince that Banbho, one of his associates wished to speak to him most urgently. The prince was unwilling to leave the Madu girl, but he could not refuse so grave a message, especially as Banbho was not only the wickedest but by far the wisest of his evil companions. The prince went out, locked the door behind him, and took Banbho into another room. The news Banbho brought was of the gravest." "The news I bring, my Prince, he said slowly," is as bad as it can be. Unless you act at once this palace of yours is certain to become your prison. The late king was angry with you, as you know, and before he died, he had engraved as his will on a brass plate that you were never to sit on the throne. In your stead the ministers were to put your son if you had one, and if not, your distant cousin. Now that a son has been born to the princess, think what a handle your enemies will have against you! They will put you in prison and make your infant son king of Brahmanabad. You must act at once!" Banbho's plan was simple. It was to proclaim the prince as king in Brahmanabad and then to gallop with every available man to Depur where the ministers had assembled to carry out the late king's wishes. Banbho taking some men with him, first rode through the streets of Brahmanabad, shouting "Victory to Dalu Rai Maharaj!" The crowd at once caught up the cry and were soon shouting "Victory to Dalu Rai Maharaj" through every lane and byway in the city. This done, Banbho returned to the prince's palace and he and the prince and his companions and all the guards whom they could muster, set off together at headlong speed for Depur. While Banbho was thus rousing his master to action, the prime-minister and the commander-in-chief and the principal nobles of Brahmanabad were seated together in one of the council rooms of Depur. The prime-minister, respected above all for his age and wisdom and for his faithful service of the late king, put before his colleagues the brass plate of king Amrai and proposed that they should take instant steps to seize the person of Dalu Rai and put his newly born son on the throne. Several of the nobles objected strongly. For all their respect for the late king and their dislike of Dalu Rai, they disliked still more the coronation of a newly born infant with all the dangers of a long regency. While they were in high debate, the commander-in-chief heard a noise in the courtyard and guessing its cause, said with a smile and a shrug of his shoulders : " I am afraid we are too late, gentlemen. The prince has come in person to settle the succession." Dalu Rai and Banbho followed by their troopers rushed up the stairs and Banbho knocking at the door, demanded entrance in the king's name. Receiving no answer, he caught up a heavy pickaxe and with a single blow broke open the lock. The door flew open and the prince and his men rushed in. Many of the nobles at once joined him. But the chief minister and a few others remained seated. As the prince stepped forward, the prime-minister gave him the brass plate on which was engraved his father's will. The prince read it and glowing with rage " from his topknot to his toenails," rushed at the old man. Both sides drew their swords. A fight ensued, but it was soon over. The prime-minister and the commander-in-chief lay dead on the ground and the rest surrendered.

Dalu Rai would at once have gone back to the Madu maiden ; but Banbho who " had a crow's wisdom " prevailed on him to spend the day and the following night on the late king's funeral ceremonies. All day long and all that night Dalu Rai's thoughts were far away with his unhappy captive. Next morning Banbho pressed him to hold a Darbar and win over the state officers and townspeople by concessions and gifts. But Dalu Rai could restrain himself no longer. "You spoiler of pleasure!" he cried angrily to Banbho, "I am not going to hold a Darbar! Tell my officers that I am too stricken with sorrow to hold one." With these words king Dalu Rai left Banbho to manage as best he could, and rode off with all speed to the conquest of the Madu maiden. Unluckily for him, he had carelessly left behind him his dagger when summoned by Banbho. The Madu girl had picked it up and when the wicked king would have caught her in his arms she pointed the dagger at him and threatened to stab him if he came near her. As he stood uncertain what to do, he heard cries outside his palace "Maharaja! Maharaja!" Dalu Rai went to the verandah and looking down saw his courtyard full of frightened people. "Maharaja, save us!" they cried. "Brahmanabad will be destroyed." Dalu Rai looked towards the horizon and saw a huge mass of sand like a tidal wave advancing on Brahmanabad. The sky was as black as pitch. The sun was hidden and the Indus had left its course and seemed to be fleeing before the sandstorm. As he gazed at the fearful scene, a voice cried: "To-day Brahmanabad shall perish because of its ruler's wickedness!" The king remembered the anchorite's curse and would have ridden away leaving his city and his people to their fate. But as he walked to the door a youth with drawn sword barred his way. "Who are you?" asked the king. "I am your death," was the grim answer. The king had no other wish but to flee from the doomed town; but the youth would not let him pass. At last the king drew his sword and the two men fought. The youth was skilled in swordmanship but even so he was no match for Dalu Rai, who was a master of the art. In a few minutes the king drove his sword through the youth's heart and bending over him dragged him into the Madu maiden's room. As he did so, the girl drove her dagger into his back. "Why did you strike me ?" asked the dying king. "Was the youth your kinsman ?" "He was my betrothed," said the girl with white lips and blazing eyes. The king fainted and life left him. The girl took some wood from the hearth where a fire was burning and lit the drapery in the room. In a few minutes it was blazing. The fire spread to the rest of the palace and it was soon a burning mass. At the same time the sand reached the walls of Brahmanabad. The burghers sought flight in all directions, but flight was useless. The sandwave caught them and stifled them, until at last there was not a living soul left in Brahmanabad.

The curse of the anchorite had been fulfilled to the letter.

THE EIGHTH KEY.

Once upon a time there ruled over Sind a king, who throughout his reign had been distinguished for wisdom and justice; but he had grown old and had only one son, born to him by one of his queens, when he was in the evening of his life. His darling wish was to see his son of an age to succeed him before he died. But as kings even are only pawns in the hands of the great chessplayer, his hope was never fulfilled. Feeling death approach, he sent for his chief minister and gave him the eight keys of his eight treasure chambers. "Guard the throne for my son" said the dying man, "and when he is of an age to rule by himself, give him seven of the eight keys ; but do not give him the eighth until he has ruled for five years." The chief minister promised faithfully to do his master's bidding and the old king died in his arms.

The young prince was duly raised to the throne and the chief minister watched over him as if he had been his own son. When the prince came of age, he succeeded to a rich and prosperous kingdom and the minister handed over to him, just as the old king had desired, seven out of the eight keys. With the seven keys the prince opened seven treasure vaults and found them chock full of silver and gold pieces and precious stones of every description. He was pleased beyond measure; and he felt deeply grateful to the faithful minister, who had discharged his trust so well and while keeping the people happy had made their king rich beyond the dreams of avarice. For a time all went well; then some evilminded old man, who envied the chief minister, told the king that there were really eight treasure vaults and that the minister had not handed over the eighth key, so that he might keep for himself the contents of the eighth treasure vault. In a great rage the young king sent for the chief minister and demanded on pain of instant death the eighth key. The old statesman fell at his young master's feet and telling him with many tears the whole story handed him the eighth key. The king was so excited at the tale, that he snatched away the key and running as fast as he could to the eighth treasure vault, turned the key in the lock and flung open the door. To his amazement the room was absolutely bare, save for the portrait of a beautiful girl, that hung on one of the walls. The king's eyes ran round the empty room and then they rested on the face in the picture. There they stayed until the youth fell so deeply in love with the beautiful girl, that he grew gradually fainter and at last swooned away. The minister and the courtiers sprinkled rosewater over their prostrate master and at last revived him; but he vowed that unless the minister promised to bring him the lovely picture maiden, he would not only refuse to reign, but would starve himself to death.

The old minister was dismayed at the state of the king and soothed him by telling him that he would at once set out to fetch the beautiful girl. He loaded a vessel full of merchandise of all descriptions and with some chosen companions weighed anchor and set sail for the open sea. They touched at various ports, but although they shewed the chief men there the portrait found in the eighth chamber, none recognised it. At last after the voyage had lasted a whole year, they reached a distant haven and there they shewed their picture. The people standing by clapped their hands and cried out "Why, it's our own princess!" The minister was taken to the king and queen who shewed them their daughter and all agreed that she was the original of the portrait. The minister told the king that he was a merchant and after giving the king splendid gifts stayed in the country until he had sold all his merchandise. He then turned his prow homewards and many months later he was able to tell his king that the lovely picture maiden had been found. Without a moment's delay the king vowed that he would seek her himself. Again filling the vessel with merchandise, the king, the minister and the same band of trusty companions went on board and weighing anchor, they set sail for the distant land wherein the princess dwelt. After a voyage of several months and many hardships, they reached it and the minister again presented himself in the guise of a merchant before the princess' father. On his earlier visit the minister had learnt that the princess was very fond of toys; so he had brought for her a number of toys, in the making of which the people of his country were very skilled. There were toy dogs that ran for miles, toy lions and tigers that roared horribly, toy partridges that rose with a whirr just like live ones, toy pheasants that flew up slantwise into the air and toymen who walked about and talked just as if they had been real. The princess gave a cry of delight on seeing all these wonderful playthings; but the minister said "These are nothing to what you will see, if you will visit our ship. My master the merchant who is on board would only let me bring the commonest toys ashore." The princess was wild to see the other toys and taking six maid-servants with her went with the minister to the seashore and aboard the ship. There the young king received her with the greatest courtesy and respect and began to shew her other toys. But as she was looking at them and clapping her hands at each fresh one, the crew quietly cut the anchor cable and were out to sea, before the princess or her friends on shore had any idea what was happening.

When the poor princess found that she had been taken captive, she wept bitterly, but the king soothed her and told her how he had fallen in love with her picture and had sailed across half the world to win her. At last she dried her eyes and promised to be his queen directly the ship brought them to his country. The journey took many weary months, but at last they were only three days sail off and the king and betrothed, as happy as possible, together were walking up and down the deck, hand in hand. The chief minister was sitting in the bows straining his eyes trying to get a glimpse of the land. Now among the old man's many accomplishments was the power to understand the speech of birds. As he looked landwards, he saw a parrot and a maina fly to the ship and perch in the rigging. After a little while the maina felt dull and begged the parrot to tell her a story. At first the parrot demurred, then he said: "There is a story going on before your very eyes. You see how happy the king and queen seem to be? Well, the king has only three more days to live! When he lands three days hence, he will be met by his officers and his troops, his elephants, his horses and his chariots. He will be given the most beautiful horse of all to ride; but that horse is not really a horse at all, but a demon. Directly the king is on its back, it will fly away with him into the air and will then drown him by flinging him into the sea." The maina was affected to tears by this story; for she loved the parrot dearly and knew how the princess would grieve at the loss of her betrothed. "Is there no way," cried the maina, "by which the king can be saved?" "Yes, my beloved," answered the parrot, "there is one way. If someone goes up to the horse just before the king mounts it and cuts its head off, the king will be saved. But do not repeat what I have told you; for if anyone repeats it, one third of his or her body will be turned into stone." The parrot and the maina then flew away, leaving the minister, who had understood all that they had said, a prey to the cruelest anxiety.

Next day the parrot and the maina flew back to the ship and perched in the rigging. The minister on seeing them went back to his seat in the bows of the ship, so that he might listen to what they said. The maina said "Tell me, please, what will happen to the king, if he escapes from the demon horse? Will he not wed the princess and live happily ever afterwards?" "Nay, my heart's desire," said the parrot, "the king and the princess will never, I fear, be happy together. Even although the king escapes from the demon horse he will still be in the gravest peril. During the wedding the king will see a beautiful gold plate. He will be so pleased with it, that he will pick it up and pass it round among his courtiers to collect alms for the Brahmans, who are conducting the ceremony. But he will not live to pass the plate to all his courtiers, for it is poisoned and as he passes it round, the poison on it will enter the pores of his skin and will kill him in a few seconds." The poor maina was as much upset at this story as she had been at the other. "Is there no way," she sobbed, "to save the poor king?" "Yes, my beloved," answered the parrot, "if anyone were to put on gloves and snatch away the plate before the king can handle it, he will be saved. But do not repeat what I have told you, for if you do, a third of your body will be turned into stone." "Shortly afterwards, the parrot and the maina flew away, leaving the minister sadder even than he had been the previous day.

The next day, which was the last of the voyage, the disheartened minister went and sat in the prow of the ship, to hear anything more that the parrot might say to the maina. He had not been seated more than a few minutes before the two birds came and perched a few feet above his head. "Dear Parrot," said the maina, "if the king is not poisoned by the plate, will he and the princess not even then marry and live happy together ever afterwards ?" "Nay, well beloved, even then the king will not live long enough to make the princess happy. After the wedding ceremony, the king and the princess will be so tired that directly their heads touch the pillow, they will go off to sleep. While they are asleep, a snake that lives in the roof of the bridal chamber will drop poison from his fangs on to the princess' cheek. When the king wakes out of his first sleep and kisses the princess, he will touch the poison with his lips and will die instantly." The maina was dreadfully sorry to hear this new danger and asked tearfully whether there was no way by which the king could escape from that death also. "Yes, well beloved," said the parrot, "there is one chance of his escape, but it is so remote that the king is sure to die. If someone were to hide himself in the bridal chamber until the poison fell and kissed the princess' cheek, the king would be saved ; nor would his saviour die either if he drank at once a large glass of milk. But do not tell anyone about this, for if you do a third of your body will be turned into stone." The two birds then flew away.

The minister was in despair, but he was a brave and loyal man and he resolved to save his master, even if it cost him his life. When the king landed and tried to mount the demon horse, the minister drew his sword and with a single stroke cut its head off. The king was very angry and asked the minister why he had done it ; but the minister dared not explain for fear of a third part of his body being turned into stone. The king could not understand it, still in view of the minister's great services he forgave him. The wedding ceremonies of the king and his bride were celebrated with great splendour ; and in the middle of them, the king seeing a beautiful gold plate stretched out his hand to take it and to collect alms for the officiating Brahmans. The minister at once pushed past the king and with a gloved hand, seized the golden plate and threw it far away into a running stream. The king was still more angry especially as the minister, afraid of being turned into stone, would not say why he had done it.

After the wedding ceremonies were over, the king and queen tired out with the fatigues of the day went to rest ; and so sleepy were they that directly their heads touched their pillows, they fell asleep. The minister, however, had hidden himself behind a screen in the bridal chamber. He saw the snake come out of his hiding place in the roof, wriggle along a beam and then drop poison on the face of the sleeping queen. He stepped up to the bed, kissed the poison off the queen's face and then took a deep draught of milk. The queen woke up on feeling the kiss and roused the king. They were both very angry at seeing the minister in their room and the king called to his guards to seize the minister and hang him early next morning from the battlements of the palace. The guards seized the poor old minister and took him to prison. There the old man asked to see the king before he died, as a last favour. The king had not the heart to refuse it. The minister was taken in chains to the royal palace and there he poured out the whole truth. But as he related how the parrot had warned him about the demon horse, his feet and legs turned to marble ; then as he told about the poisoned plate, his body as far as his armpits turned to marble ; lastly when he had finished the tale of the poison dropped by the snake, his head and shoulders became marble, too.

The king was at first too astonished to do anything and then he wept bitterly at the awful fate that had overtaken his loyal and faithful servant. He put the petrified body in a room in his palace and daily for several years prostrated himself at its feet to shew his sorrow. In course of time the queen bore him a son and every day he used to bring the little boy into the minister's room to shew him what a good and true servant he had once had. One day when the little boy was three years old, the very same parrot and maina, that had perched in the ship's rigging, flew into the minister's room and began talking to each other. The king just because he was standing close to the minister was able to follow what they were saying. The parrot said to the maina "The king is very sad at the fate of his minister ; but he could bring him back to life now, if he wanted to." "How could he ?" asked the maina. The parrot answered "If he kills his own son and sprinkles his blood over the stone body, the minister will become flesh and blood once more." The king thought long and deeply where his duty lay ; at last he felt that he owed more to the faithful minister who had saved his life three times than to his son. He drew his sword, cut off the little boy's head and sprinkled his blood over the marble body. The minister at once came to life again. Nor was this all. The minister learning of the death of the little prince prayed so earnestly to God to bring him back to life that his prayer was granted. The king then took the minister and the little prince to the queen's room and told her all that had happened. She agreed that the king had acted rightly, even though his act would but for God's mercy, have cost her her son. The minister once more resumed his duties ; and he and the king, the queen and the little prince lived together happily for ever so long afterwards.

THE NOOSE OF MURAD.

Near the small town of Naushahro in the district of Nawabshah, there is an old fort called Murad jo Killo or Murad's Fort. It is a big place, but crumbling to ruins ; still the walls that remain are so wide that three men, so it is said, can sleep on them side by side. There is also in that part of the country a proverbial saying, used when anyone grumbles at his lot, "Does he want Murad jo phaho" (the noose of Murad). Now this is the tale that is told both of the fort and of the proverbial saying:

Somewhere in the early part of the eighteenth century, when Nur Mahomed Kalhoro was ruler of Sind, he had as jamadar or headman of his grass-cutters a certain Murad, known as Murad Ganjo or Murad the Bald. So completely had his hair vanished, that you might have looked all over his head from north to south and from east to west and then any other way you liked, but you would not have found a single hair on any part of it. Murad used daily to inspect the grass-cutters' work and when on this duty, he noticed an old half mad-woman called Fatima. For some days he paid no attention to her. Then it occurred to him that the old woman might be a witch or sorceress, whom it might be well to propitiate ; so he reverently went up to her and asked for her blessing. The old woman looked at him attentively and then blessed him, adding

"Murad the Bald, you will become a kardar," or as we should say nowadays a tapedar or talati. Murad thought no more about the prophecy until one day Nur Mahomed Kalhoro, in return for Murad's honesty and hard work, promoted him from jamadar of grass-cutters to be a kardar.

Murad was now quite certain that the old woman was a real sorceress, one to be made much of in every way. For many months he brought her daily small gifts of food or money; then he summoned up courage to ask again for her blessing. Again the old woman looked at him intently, blessed him and added "Murad the Bald, you will be a naib subha," or as we should say nowadays a Deputy Collector. Not many months passed before Nur Mahomed Kalhoro, still more pleased with Murad's steady and faithful work, promoted him to be a Naib Subha. There is a French proverb which says *L'appétit vient en mangeant*, that is to say the greedy are never satisfied; and Murad began to feel soon that the post of Naib Subha was far beneath his merits. He plied the old woman with more valuable gifts and for the third time asked her blessing. She looked intently at him as before and blessing him for the third time said "Murad the Bald, you will become a subha" or as we should say a Collector of a district. Murad the Bald not very long afterwards was given charge of a district, thereby reaching a post far above his deserts. He was still an ignorant, unlettered boor and for a time he was fully satisfied with his office. He built the great fort known as Murad jo Killo and seemed perfectly contented. But after a year or two be began to think that the old woman, who had raised him so high, might raise him higher still, might make him a king or perhaps even emperor of Delhi. After all stranger things had happened before and "Allah alone knoweth all." Tortured by his insatiable greed, Murad the Bald showered jewels and gold on the old woman and for the fourth time asked for her blessing. But this time a terrible thing occurred. Instead of the fixed kindly look, that she had been used to give him, her eyes flashed with demoniac fury and instead of a blessing, she cursed him " Murad the Bald," she screamed at him " you will rise higher still, you will be hanged." Poor Murad left the witch as she raved and gnashed her teeth and going home, tried in vain to put the matter out of his mind.

Now it so happened that the Afghan ruler of Multan, Nadir Khan by name, lost the youngest and most beautiful of his wives. She fell in love with one of her lord's servants and ran away with him right out of the Multan province into Murad's district. She took with her a huge diamond and a priceless manuscript on surgery and medicine. Murad the Bald came to hear of the arrival of the two fugitives and promptly took from them the diamond and the manuscript, which he stored in the royal treasure house of Nur Mahomed Kalhoro. The queen and her lover, fearing that they might themselves be detained and given over to Nadir Khan, fled from Sind pretending that they were going on a pilgrimage to Mecca.

In the meantime the indignant Nadir Khan in vain looked all over his kingdom for his missing queen and servant. At last he learnt that she and her lover had fled into the lands of Nur Mahomed Kalhoro. Nadir Khan summoned his army and marching to the frontier, demanded the surrender of the queen and her lover, the diamond and the manuscript. Nur Mahomed Kalhoro enquired of Murad and learnt that the guilty couple had fled, but that the diamond and the manuscript were safe in his treasury. He sent back the manuscript and the diamond. " These came into our hands," he wrote, " but they do not belong to us. The guilty couple have fled, so we cannot return them, but take the manuscript and the diamond since they are yours. We do not want them nor do we wish for war. Nevertheless, if you are bent on war, we shall accept your challenge. We shall gladly shew you how strong are our arms and how sharp are our swords."

Nadir Khan liked Nur Mahomed's answer and instead of war there was peace, and instead of battles and skirmishes there were visits and reviews and banquets. Nevertheless Nadir the Afghan was not quite sure that Nur Mahomed Kalhoro had not seized his beautiful queen and hidden her in some deep recess of his own harem. He sent for Murad and begged him to speak the truth: "If my queen and servant have really gone to Mecca, it is useless to search for them here; but if Nur Mahomed Kalhoro is secretly keeping my queen, then I shall slay him and give his throne to the man, who tells me the whole truth." As Murad listened to the words of the Afghan, Satan the Stoned seized his five senses. Forgetting all his master's kindness and favours, he thought to himself that there now stretched in front of him an open and easy road to a throne. With seeming reluctance he confessed that the queen and her paramour had never left Sind. Nur Mahomed Kalhoro had taken the queen to be his concubine and had cut off the head of her paramour with a single stroke of his sword, just as if he had been a buffalo. Nadir the Afghan believing Murad and angry at what he believed to be the double dealing of Nur Mahomed Kalhoro, resolved to march into Sind and to seat Murad on the throne in his place. He had gone only one march when the news reached him that his missing queen and her lover had been found in the country of a neighbouring Raja, who was sending them back in chains to their master,

Nadir the Afghan was now as angry with Murad as he had been with Nur Mahomed Kalhoro. He told the latter the lying tale told by his subha Murad. Mahomed Nur was shocked at the ingratitude of the base born wretch on whom he had lavished favours. His horsemen rode out and seized Murad the Bald and at the king's orders, hanged him from the battlements of his own fortress. So ended the fortunes of the greedy and faithless adventurer ; and that is why men say to-day that it is better to be contented with one's lot than to rise so high that in the end one dangles from the end of a rope forty or fifty feet above the ground.

THE MAKLI HILL.

Most English visitors to Tatta go there for the shooting only and I should be the last to blame them. Below the ancient fort of Kalankot near Tatta is a lake of the same name. It is quite shallow and overgrown with tall reeds, the home of innumerable duck. They rise all round, as one is poled in boats through lanes cut among the reeds and quick eye and hand are needed before they can be bagged. But close to the bungalow are a number of ancient tombs ; and as no record of their owners is to be found on the walls, a few facts about them may prove interesting to future visitors.

The tombs are built on a ridge known as the Makli Hill. Two derivations of the name are given. Some say that the hill owes its title to a pious woman called Makli who lived and was buried on it. Others say that a holy man gave it the name of Makli because he deemed it Maka laali or the threshold of Mecca. Whatever the true origin may be, let us take the tombs from north to south and put down what we know about them. The farthest to the north is a brick tomb on a masonry plinth, plastered and white-washed. Beneath it lie the earthly remains of Sayad Ali Shirazi. Great saint though he was, he would long ago have been forgotten, save for the fact that for a moment his career touched that of the great Akbar. The Emperor Humayun, defeated in battle after battle by the great Afghan soldier Sher Shah, fled to Sind. After trying in vain to establish himself at Sehwan and Bukkur, he started for Bikanir, only to learn that the Chief meant to hand him over to his enemy. He turned back and made his way first to Jasalmir and then through the desert to Umarkot. Most of his companions died of thirst. The others losing in their misery all respect for their leader, let him walk so that his wife, Akbar's mother, should ride. At last with only seven attendants he reached Umarkot and there on the 14th October 1542 Akbar was born. Humayun had neither gifts to distribute to his friends nor clothes in which to wrap the baby. The first difficulty he overcame by breaking a pod of musk and letting its perfume spread among his guests, at the same time exclaiming with prophetic truth that his baby boy's fame would diffuse itself through the world like the fragrance of the musk. The second difficulty he met by cutting Akbar's first garment out of the coat of Sayad Ali Shirazi, who had been sent by the people of Tatta with gifts and greetings. Ali Shirazi lived for thirty years afterwards and the date of his burial is inscribed on his tomb, *viz.*, 1752 A.D.

South of the Sayad's tomb is that of Makli, the eponymous heroine of the hill, and south of Makli's is that of Jam Nindo. It is easily distinguished as it has no roof and its stones were evidently taken from some ancient Hindu temple. Jam Nindo or the Little Jam was the founder of Tatta. His real name was Jam Nizam-ud-din and he was a Samma by caste. Here we must go back into early Sind History. When the Afghan

Emperor Ala-ud-din Khilji conquered Sind, a Rajput tribe named the Sumras were in possession. Subdued then, they successfully revolted in the reign of Ghazi-ud-din Tughlak. In the middle of the 14th century, however, they were ousted by another Rajput tribe the Sammas. The latter ruled Sind from 1350 A.D. to 1521 A.D. But until Jam Nindo's time they did not live at Tatta. They lived at Samui three miles to the northwest. When Jam Nindo had established his power and cleared the land of robbers, he thought he would build a new town, " wherein happiness might remain for ever." He chose a site to the east of the Makli Hill and on a day picked out by the Brahmans, he founded his city, Tatta There he ruled for at least fifty years and was buried on the Makli Hill. Another Samma chief buried there was Jam Tamachi. He was the Jam who loved the fisher maiden Nuri and was the ancestor of the Jadeja Raos of Cutch. But it is not possible to say with certainty which his tomb is ! *

Jam Nindo's son and successor was Jam Feroz. But the new Jam loved too warmly the beauty of his dancing girls and the jokes of his jesters to be a good ruler. The result was that in 1521 A.D. he was driven from his throne by Shahbeg Arghun, who had himself been driven from Kandahar by the lion hearted Babar. In 1536 A.D. Shah Hussein Arghun succeeded his father Shahbeg and was the ruler of Sind when Humayun fled to it and Akbar was born. In 1554 he died and Mirza Isa Tarkhan, the founder of the Tarkhan Dynasty, became master of Tatta. It is to his tomb to which we come, shortly after saying goodbye to Jam Nindo's. Isa Khan's last dwelling place stands in a large courtyard close to an old

---

*For the story of Jam Tamachi and Nuri, see "Tales of Old Sind" (Oxford University Press).

mosque. The tomb is entirely of carved stone with perforated slabs let in here and there. It was in Mirza Isa's time that the Portuguese sacked Tatta. It seems that in 1555 Mirza Isa Khan quarrelled with Sultan Mahmud the Governor of Bukkur by whose aid he had become King of Sind. Isa Khan sent an envoy to Goa to ask help from the Portuguese. The fame of that nation in India was then at its height. Only a few years before they had helped the King of Guzarat to drive out Humayun and in return had received Bassein and the whole Province of the north including Salsette Island. With their aid Isa Khan felt sure that he could humble Sultan Mahmud. On the other hand, no doubt, the Portuguese Governor-General dreamed visions of a second northern province on the banks of the Indus. He sent a fleet of 28 ships with 700 men under Pedro Baretto. The gallant Pedro duly sailed up the Indus and reaching Tatta asked for orders. In the meantime, however, Isa Khan had in several actions instilled into Sultan Mahmud Khan a sense of his inferiority and had forced him to sue for peace. Isa Khan sent word from Bukkur that he no longer needed Portuguese help. Pedro then asked for the cost of the expedition, estimated, I dare say, on a liberal scale. Isa Khan politely refused to pay. Dom Pedro flew into a rage, sacked Tatta, killed 800 people, took away two millions sterling and left the town in flames. Isa Khan rebuilt the town but he entered into no more alliances with the Portuguese. He ruled prosperously until 1572 A. D. when he died and was buried on the Makli Hill.

On Isa Khan's death his son Mahomed Baki succeeded him. His tomb is a small ruined brick enclosure, the one immediately to the north of Tural Beg's, of whom I shall say a word or two later. Isa Khan's tomb is a poor thing compared with his father's and his son's, but then so was Mahomed Baki himself. For twelve years he gave the good people of Tatta a dreadful time. To slit their ears and noses and shave off their beards was the favourite pastime of his leisure moments. To hang them, impale them and throw them under the feet of his elephants was the serious business of his life. At last in 1584, having lived to see his daughter returned with thanks by the Emperor Akbar, he committed suicide. To him succeeded his son Jani Beg, whose tomb is the southern most of all. It is of brick, faced with glazed blue and green tiles. It has a perforated window above the door and there are geometric tracery windows also on the four sides. By the time Jani Beg had succeeded his father, the genius of Akbar was at its zenith. Sultan Mahmud of Bukkur yielded to the great Emperor his sovereignty without a blow. But Jani Beg was of sterner stuff. Entrenching himself behind the river Phito, he withstood for some months the imperial forces. Driven from his trenches he fell back on the great fort of Kalankot; but that Akbar should not use Tatta as his base, he destroyed it and left the emperor a smouldering ruin. Yet brave as he was, he had at last to kiss the stirrup of the world conqueror, was graciously received and confirmed as imperial governor of Tatta. He died there in 1599. The Emperor confirmed in his place his son Ghazi Beg. The latter lived until 1612,when he was murdered. His body was buried in the same tomb as Jani Beg and the common grave was for many years the scene of a curious pilgrimage. Both father and son were renowned as poets and musicians and childless couples who desired off-spring, used to visit their tomb and try and win the favour of their spirits by songs and instruments. But efficacious as his spiritual aid may have been in procuring sons for barren women, poor Ghazi remained childless himself. He had no son and with him the Tarkhan dynasty of Sind ended.

The Moghul emperors thereafter ruled Sind through governors appointed directly from Delhi. The Tomb of Diwan Shurfa Khan, the minister of one of these governors, Amirkhan by name, is one of the best preserved on Makli Hill. Another less well preserved, but even more imposing tomb, that of Nawab Isa Khan, dates from the same period A. D. 1628-1644. It has an upper storey to which leads a flight of stairs. To the east of Isa Khan's tomb are the graves of the ladies of his ample Zanana. To the south of Isakhan's tomb is quite a small one, that of Mirza Tural Beg. It appears that he misused his position by artificially forcing up the price of grain and then selling his stock at a large profit. He was so hated in his lifetime that he took the precaution to build his own tomb. But even so he did not escape infamy. He was nicknamed the " Dukario " or " Famine Man " and every one who passed his grave used regularly to heave a stone at it. In time the stones were piled up right to the stone canopy above it. Fortunately for the " Famine Man " the Public Works Department have taken charge of his tomb and have removed the stones. But his memory is still detested and his present address is believed to be somewhere in the very centre of the flaming halls of Iblis.

LARKANA.

A few miles from Larkana at a place called Fatehpur is a handsome mosque. In its courtyard hang innumerable bells. I long tried in vain to learn its history but at last I obtained from Mr. Bherumal, Inspector of Excise, the following legend.

The town of Larkana derives its name from the tribe of Larak and was probably at one time called *Larakanjo got* or the village of the Larak tribesmen. They were followers of a family known to history as the Kalhoras, whose family name Abbassi lent strength to their claim that they were sprung from the loins of Abbas, the uncle of the holy Prophet. After the conquest of Sind by Akbar, it became a province of the Moghul empire; but with the decline of the imperial power, authority relaxed and disorder grew. Of this disorder the Kalhoras took advantage. The first great Kalhoro was Adam Shah, who "drank the sherbet of martyrdom at Multan" or in simpler language was killed in an obscure fight with the Moghul governor of that city. Adam Shah's grandson Shahlal Mahomed was the famous saint, whose memory still lives in the Fatehpur mosque. His first and perhaps greatest—certainly his most useful—miracle was the digging of the Ghar canal that runs past Larkana town. He did not dig it with a spade. His methods were simpler and more efficient. He mounted a *Kando* or thorn tree. Once firmly seated in its upper branches, he made the wretched vegetable drag its roots from Larkana to Kambar, a distance of twelve miles. In the deep hollow caused by the progress of the *Kando* tree, flowed the obedient water. The stream so created came to be known as the Shahlal Wah or the canal of Shahlal Mahomed. Many years later Mian Nur Mahomed Kalhoro widened the Shahlal Wah and changed its name to Ghar canal, *i.e.*, the canal broken by the tree driven by the Saint's superhuman powers. The Ghar canal bears this name to the present day and the tree which Shahlal Mahomed used as his humble instrument is still pointed out on the bank of the Chilo canal in the Kambar taluka.

The miracle of the Ghar canal was followed by so many others that the imperial governor became alarmed at the Saint's growing fame and power. He reported the facts to Aurangzeb and obtained that emperor's leave to shorten Shahlal Mahomed's stature by a head. After a mighty resistance the Saint was taken captive and executed. The governor put his head in a wooden box and sealing it sent it in charge of a police guard to the emperor's camp. When the police guard reached Lahore they out of curiosity opened the box, in order to see what the head looked like. The lid was no sooner lifted than the head flew out and made its way through the air to Shahlal Mahomed's favourite village of Fatehpur, wherein the Saint's body lay buried. The police guard were so alarmed at the strange behaviour of the head that they dared neither return to Larkana nor go on to Delhi. They buried the empty box in Lahore and building a shrine over it, appointed themselves its guardians.

The emperor, however, who was eagerly expecting the sealed box, got disturbed at its delay. He sent a body of troops to Lahore to find out what had happened to it. At first they could find out nothing. At last hearing of the new shrine, they went there and extorted from its guardians the whole truth. They then dug up the ground and unearthed the box. Opening it they found it, not only to their own amazement but to that of the quondam police guard, by no means empty. It contained another head of Shahlal Mahomed exactly similar to the one that had flown away. The troops carried away box and head and showed them to Aurangzeb. Convinced of the miracle, the devout emperor felt sure that he had killed a Saint. To show his repentance of his cruel deed, he had a tomb built at Delhi over the box and the head. In the meantime, the Larak tribe and the other countless disciples of Shahlal Mahomed had built the mosque at Fatehpur over the holy man's body and true head, once more in union. Thus the great saint is honoured by no less than three tombs, one at Fatehpur, where lie his real head and body, a second at Lahore where the empty box was buried and disinterred, and a third at Delhi where the second head lies.

The descendants of Shahlal Mahomed were the famous Kalhoro Mirs who ruled Sind until overthrown by the Talpurs. Their capital was Haidarabad but they always loved Larkana for the sake of their ancestor ; and the fame of its prosperity and wealth under the Kalhoros is still preserved in the well-known couplet

Hujie Nano

Ta gumh Larkano

If you have money (to spend) then go to Larkana.

TWO LOVE TRAGEDIES.

KUTTEJI KABAR AND MAUSUM SHAH.

One of the highest peaks of the Baluch mountains along the frontier of the Larkana district is known as the Kutteji kabar. This is the tale they tell about it. Once upon a time a rich Brohi hillman owned a very faithful and obedient dog. The Brohi was at one time rich, but from one cause or another he lost his wealth and of all his riches nothing was left to him but his dog. One day when he had no money left, he mortgaged his dog for a hundred rupees to a bania of the neighbourhood. Before leaving it, he bade his hound serv itse new master as faithfully as it had served him. The dog wagged its tail as if it fully understood what the hillman told him.

Several months passed by and the dog was as obedient to the bania as it had been to the Brohi. One night a band of fierce robbers broke into the house of the bania, over-powered the inmates and carried off the savings of the merchant's lifetime. After the robbers had left, the bania began to mourn and beat his breast. In an hour or so the dog came to him and tugged at his coat. The bania abused and beat it for not having guarded him against the robbers. But the dog continued so to pull at his coat, that the neighbours advised him to go with the dog and see what it wanted. The dog led by the way for a mile or so until it came to a torrent bed, when it began to dig in the ground with its paws. The bania and his neighbours also began to dig ; at last they came upon the bania's safe with his money secure inside it. The dog seeing that it could not fight with success against a band of armed robbers, waited until they had left and then followed them until it saw them conceal their plunder. Then it went back to tell the bania. The latter was so touched at the dog's fidelity and sense that he tied round its neck a letter to the Brohi. In it he told his debtor that he cancelled his debt and asked him to take his dog back free of incumbrances. Then he told the dog to go back to its master. Off it went wagging its tail and barking delightedly at the thought of seeing its old master.

Now it so chanced that the Brohi hillman had by working in the plains saved a sum sufficient to pay off his debt and he was returning to the hills to do so. On the way he met his hound. It rushed towards him in a transport of joy. But the hillman who knew nothing of the dog's conduct and did not notice the letter round its neck, thought that it had disgraced him by running away from his creditor before he had paid his debt. A man of high honour, he grew very angry and holding out the fingers of his right hand made the *bhundo* sign in the dog's face. This deadly and contemptuous insult was too much for the poor dog. It fell at its master's feet and died on the spot. The Brohi tried in vain to bring it back to life. As he tried, he saw the bania's letter round its neck and learnt too late how innocent the dead dog had been. In his grief, he bore the dog's body to the highest peak of the neighbouring mountains and buried it there. For some time he remained by the tomb as its majawar or guardian. Then he sickened and died also. But the peak is still known as Kutteji kabar.

. Another love story of a different kind is told of the minaret of Mausum Shah, that looks down from a great height on the thriving town of Sukkur and the splendid river Indus, as it runs through its two limestone banks. A certain Musulman called Mausumshah fell in love with one of the bania girls of Sukkur, whose beauty is renowned through all Sind. But he was a Musulman and the lady was a Hindu. The lady would not join Islam and he could not, if he would, become a Hindu. Yet unless one or the other became a convert, marriage between them was impossible. The lady moreover had little liking for her Musulman wooer, although perhaps a little flattered by his pressing attentions. To be rid of his ardent importunities, she bade him build a minaret, two hundred feet high before he aspired to her hand. But she had not realised the passion of the unhappy Mausum Shah. He set to work, collected stones and coolies and before the Hindu lady was very much older, she saw to her horror a splendid minaret rising above the ground. In a few more months it was finished and Mausum Shah full of pride and love went to claim the hand of his beloved. But as Francis the First, an experienced judge of the fair sex, used to say "Souvent femme varie, fol qui s'y fie," and the lady proved as untractable as ever. In spite of her former implied promise she still refused to wed a circumcised barbarian. "I did not say that I would marry you," she said "when you had finished the minaret. I only wanted you to build it that you might throw yourself from the top!" Cruelty could go no further; and the broken-hearted lover ascending the minaret, took a last view of the splendid panorama unrolled before his eyes and plunged head first from the pinnacle. Legend, however, relates that he never struck the ground, nor was he dashed to pieces. A divine hand caught him as he fell and put him safely on his feet. His love for the beautiful Hindu girl had died within him. He had seen the selfish heart that beat within her beautiful body. Giving up the things of this world, he became an anchorite and taught the precepts of Islam until death overtook him. He was buried at the foot of the tower from which he had once thrown himself. And to this day his tomb and those of his disciples may be seen there by the visitor to Sukkur.

SWAMI VANKHANDI OF SADH BELO.

The early history of Sadh Belo is closely connected with that of the famous Swami Vankhandi. Swami Vankhandi had been incarnated once in the seventeenth century, for we find him receiving worship as early as 1710. We, however, are only concerned with his second incarnation, which occurred in or about A. D. 1764. In the later descent on earth he lived and practised yog or asceticism at Muran Jharee in the territory of H. H. The Maharaja of Nepal. While he was still a young man his reputation for holiness spread far and wide; but it aroused the envy and malice of another anchorite of Muran Jharee named Gusai Sanyasi Sadhu. At last Gusai could contain himself no longer and made his way to the court of the Maharaja. There he told his sovereign that a certain sadhu of Muran Jharee had vowed by his austerities to destroy the kingdom. He warned the Maharaja that for several months the Sadhu had touched neither food nor water and he begged his master to destroy the Sadhu before it was too late. The Maharaja was alarmed and sent an army to take prisoner the seditious anchorite and bring him to Khatmandu, the chief town of Nepal.

When the army appeared at Muran Jharee, they found Swami Vankhandi absorbed in contemplation. As they watched him their own warlike spirit ebbed away and they were filled with a great calm; without saying a word they waited until the Swami thought fit to lift his eyes towards them. The Nepal General then told the Swami that he had received orders to take him prisoner and humbly implored his pardon. The Swami forgave him and told him that he would go on ahead of the army and wait for them at Khatmandu. With these words the Swami vanished and although the General and his officers searched for him everywhere, they could not find him. At last they returned to Khatmandu and just outside the walls, they found the Swami sitting in a deep religious trance, in the shade of a banian tree. They did not disturb him but went straight to the Maharaja, to whom they told all that had happened. The Maharaja saw that he had been deceived by the wicked Gusai and drove him from the town; then he asked for the pardon and blessing of Swami Vankhandi. The Swami saw that the Maharaja had truly repented and forgave and blessed him. Then he vanished and in the twinkling of an eye was once more to be seen at his own place in Muran Jharee.

Many and great were the miracles recorded of Swami Vankhandi, but the one that will interest English readers most is the summary way in which he dealt with a certain Captain Pauk Wales, a gentleman whom I have not been able to trace in English works of reference. In 1822 Swami Vankhandi after many pilgrimages to the holy shrines of India came to Sind, Cholera was then raging in Haidarabad, but the Swami's presence proved sufficient to drive it away. From Haidarabad he went to Khairpur and Rohri and seeing Sadh Belo island in the river Indus near Sukkur resolved to settle there and found a monastery. There he lived for twenty years until such time as Sir Charles

Napier conquered Sind and appointed Captain Pauk Wales as Collector of the Shikarpur district. Captain Pauk Wales, wholly ignorant of the power and fame of the Swami, thought that Sadh Belo island would be an ideal place for a collector's bungalow. With Captain Pauk Wales, action followed swiftly on the heels of thought. He sent for masons and building materials and began to build a bungalow. But every morning that he went to look at the work, he found that during the night it had been levelled with the ground. He was convinced that the masons and the Swami were acting in collusion and he set a guard of English soldiers over Sadh Belo. Although the soldiers never closed their eyes all night, Captain Pauk Wales next day found that not only had the masonry work been thrown down in the night, but that the bricks, mortar and all the building materials collected by him had vanished. In a rage he went up to the Swami and roundly abused him. While Captain Pauk Wales was swearing horribly, the Swami, shocked beyond measure, vanished into thin air. That night both Captain Pauk Wales and his wife were seized with internal pains of an agonising description. After a night of anguish Mrs. Pauk Wales advised her lord and master to beg the Swami's pardon. For a long time the Swami could not be found, but with the aid of the townspeople, he was eventually traced to a spot outside Sukkur, where he was quietly singing to himself. Captain Pauk Wales threw himself at the Swami's feet and promised never more to interfere with his holy island.

Swami Vankhandi lived on to the ripe age of a hundred. Feeling himself nigh to death, he sent for his disciples and warned them of his approaching end. He told them that he would hold his breath until his soul departed. When they thought him dead, they should put a pat of butter on his forehead. If it did not melt, it meant that he had ceased to live. They should then throw his corpse into the Indus river. The disciples faithfully carried out their master's wishes and when the pat of butter did not melt on his forehead, they threw his body into the great river. They had barely done so, when a rich merchant of Shikarpur came to Sadh Belo with a precious necklace of pearls for Vankhandi, of whose death he was unaware. Learning that Vankhandi was no more, the merchant refused to return to Shikarpur and infinitely firm of purpose, he vowed to sit by the edge of the river and neither to eat nor to drink until the Swami came himself to accept the necklace. On the second night the Swami in a dream promised that he would appear before his devoted follower the next day. Fortified by the vision, the Shikarpur merchant sat on by the edge of the stream. At noon the body of the Swami rose out of the Indus and the merchant put the necklace round its neck. The body then lay on the bank and the merchant called to him the anchorites of the place, who once more consigned reverently the body of the Saint into the whirling waters of the mighty river.

GUZARAT FOLK STORIES.

GUZARAT FOLK STORIES—I.

KING MANSING OF SIROHI.

King Mansing of Sirohi was a very brave Rajput ; but he had one fault. He was greatly addicted to opium, of which he used to drink daily vast quantities from the hand of his favourite queen. Now it so happened that the Emperor of Delhi came to Rajputana and camped outside the walls of Sirohi. All night long the emperor and his nobles drank deep and revelled, while beautiful dancing girls sang to them lascivious songs. The noise of the music and the dancing could be heard from king Mansing's palace ; and all one night, as the king slept, his favourite queen sat up and listened to it. When Mansing awoke, his queen gave him his opium. As he drank it, she talked about the wonderful revels of the emperor and the noise of his music and the lights that blazed all night in his camp. At first Mansing paid no heed to his queen's chatter ; but at last he got cross and told her not to mention in his presence the name of the Mleccha emperor. The queen was so infatuated with what she had seen and heard that she would not stop, but began to compare the gaiety of the emperor's camp with the dulness of life in Sirohi. At last the king lost all patience and boxing his wife's ears told her that if she thought so much of the emperor's camp, she had better go there.

The queen left the room in a rage and all that day brooded over the king's words. That night she took her maid with her and stole out of the palace and through the city walls into the emperor's camp. When she reached his tent, she sent her maid to tell the emperor. He was listening to the singing of his dancing girls and the music of his players ; but as soon as he learnt that the queen was outside, he stopped the music and the singing and had the queen brought before him with the greatest respect. As she entered the tent the whole company rose and greeted her. The emperor asked her why she had come. She replied "Grant me a boon, shelter of the world, and I shall tell you." The emperor replied " The boon is yours ; you have but to name it." The queen told the emperor all that had happened and claimed as a boon that the emperor should marry her. After she had spoken, she took the emperor's cup in her hands and drank from it, thus breaking her caste in the sight of all. The emperor had no wish to quarrel with king Mansing of Sirohi, but having made the queen a promise, he had to keep it. He called the kazi and married the queen. The same night he left Sirohi and marched back to Delhi.

The king had seen the queen leave his room in a rage, but he thought no more of the matter until next morning, when she did not come with his opium. He sent for her ; but as she did not come he called her maids and forced from their trembling lips the truth. The king said nothing, but swallowing a prodigious quantity of opium, he put on his armour and summoned his chiefs and nobles. When they had assembled, he told them that the emperor had seduced his queen and then like a coward had run away to Delhi. The chiefs and nobles all vowed vengeance and bade the king call out his troops. At noon the king held a great parade ; but when he came to count his warriors, he found that they barely numbered 6,000. On hearing this, the king's minister Motishah told him that he could do nothing with only 6,000 men against the 120,000 men led by the emperor. " What then can I do ? " cried the king. " Let us go to Delhi in disguise," said Motishah. " There we shall be able to hit on some plan to win back the queen." The king agreed ; and disguising themselves as two Rajput soldiers, he and Motishah rode from Sirohi to Delhi. At Delhi they put up with a mali woman, who worked in the imperial gardens. From her they learnt that the emperor fearing a rescue, had dug round the queen's palace no less than seven trenches. Of these six were filled with water and the inner one with fire. Outside the trenches he had built a mighty wall.

That night the king and Motishah disguised as mendicants, but with swords and shields hidden beneath their yellow robes sallied forth to the queen's palace. On coming to the wall, Motishah climbed on to the king's shoulders and thence on to the wall. He let down his turban and by its means hauled the king after him. As both could swim, they easily crossed the six water trenches. They had hoped to find the fire-trench burning low at night. But the king's guards before going home had filled it with fresh wood and it was burning fiercely. Motishah threw his shield into the middle and jumped on to it. But so great was the heat that he soon felt that his legs would be burnt off. So keeping his right leg on the shield, he kept his left leg as high as he could, to save it from the flames. He supported himself on his spear while the king sprang on his shoulders and leapt to the far side of the trench. Near the palace was a tall palm tree. Mansing climbed it and reaching the top, tied his turban to one of the branches. He then swung on his turban to and fro until he was able to swing into one of the windows of the upper storey of the palace. He tied his turban to the window sill and went inside. In a room close by he saw his queen sleeping with the emperor. At first he felt so angry that he would have killed them both, as they slept. Then he remembered that he was a Rajput and that it was wrong to kill a helpless enemy. So he woke the queen and with the point of his sword at her throat, he made her get up without waking the emperor. Tying a rope round her arms and legs and throwing her like a bundle across his back, he swung back to the palm tree by his turban and slid to the ground.

Poor Motisah's right leg was by this time all but burnt off; but when he saw the king coming back he put his left leg on the shield and over his shoulders the king climbed across the fire trench. But he could not save his minister. No sooner had Mansing reached safety than poor Motishah fainted and falling into the trench was burnt to ashes. Mansing swam with his queen on his back across the six water trenches. By the aid of Motishah's turban, which still hung from the wall, he climbed over it and pulled his wife after him. He seated her on his horse and mounting Motishah's mare, galloped off towards Sirohi. When they had ridden some fifty miles, Mansing stopped to have his morning dose of opium. He then discovered for the first time that he had dropped his opium box inside the emperor's palace. Addicted as he was to the drug, he could do without food, but he could not do without his opium. It would have been useless for him to ride further, for he would have fallen off the saddle. After stamping on the ground several times with rage, he tied his queen to a tree. Then he lay down on the ground and covering his head with a sheet fell asleep.

In the meantime the emperor had awakened and had missed the Sirohi queen. He asked his guards and his servants and searched everywhere for her but in vain. Then his eyes fell on Mansing's gold opium box. He picked it up and saw engraved on it the name "Mansing." He summoned to him his nobles and called for a volunteer to chase Mansing and bring him back alive. A Musulman noble famed for his courage rose, saluted the emperor and promised to bring the king back alive.

He galloped towards Sirohi and after riding 50 miles overtook the king and queen. Mansing still lay asleep. The Musulman noble untied the queen but he refused to kill Mansing, although she begged him to. He must bring him back alive, the Musulman said. He would give the king opium and then take him back to Delhi. "If you give him opium," said the queen, "you will never take him alive, he will kill you." The Musulman did not heed her, but mixing opium with water he poured it down Mansing's throat. Directly Mansing recovered his senses, he refused to go back to Delhi. He sprang on his horse and fought the Musulman. But Mansing was still faint from his long privation and the Musulman disarmed him and tied him to a tree. Leaving the queen to guard her husband the Musulman went down the steps of a well to wash his face and hands. The queen seeing her chance, picked up Mansing's sword as it lay on the ground and struck a blow at his head. Mansing jerked his head aside. The blade missed his head and grazing his side cut through the rope which bound him. In a moment he was free. Rushing at the queen, he twisted the sword from her hand and tied her to the tree. He mixed himself some more opium. Then arming himself with sword and shield, he went to the mouth of the well and challenged the Musulman to a second fight. The Musulman came out of the well, but now that Mansing had had his full dose of opium, no one in the world could have beaten him. With a single sweep of his sword he severed the Musulman's head from his body. Then tying his wife's hands and feet to her horse, he rode back with her in triumph to Sirohi. There all the nobles and common people rejoiced at the king's feat of arms and were very angry with the queen, who had first left him and then had tried to kill him. Mansing had her tied to a pillar in the market place. There everyone threw bricks and stones at her or hit her head with their shoes. She soon died and her body was burnt outside the city walls.

The emperor was very angry when he heard that Mansing had killed the brave Musulman noble. He raised a great army and marched against Sirohi. Yet small though the Sirohi army was, it won repeated victories over the Moghul troops. At last the emperor challenged the king to a duel, but the emperor was no match for the Rajput king. He was soon wounded and disarmed. As the price of his life, he agreed to make a treaty by which he gave great wealth and wide lands to the king of Sirohi.

GUZARAT FOLK STORIES—II.

THE WISDOM SELLER.

Once upon a time there lived a poor Brahman, who earned a tiny income as a clerk. He had one son, a bright, clever boy, who went to school and was a favourite alike of boys and masters. He might have risen to great learning, had his father lived. Unhappily before the boy had left school the poor Brahman died. The boy had to leave school and try to keep his mother and younger brothers and sisters. At first he became a candidate for a clerkship in a public office. But this brought him no pay; and although he wrote petitions in his spare time, he only earned thereby Rs. 3 or Rs. 4 a month. This sum was not enough to keep him and his family from starving. One day he resolved to seek some other way of earning a living and this is what he did.

He went into the town and hired the smallest shop he could find. He spent the few annas he had in the world in buying some writing paper, an ink pot, a bottle of ink, a pen and an empty box. Over the shop he got painted the words "WISDOM SELLER." All round him were jewellers' shops, cloth shops, green-grocers' shops. The other dealers waited for customers, but the green-grocers shouted to the passersby "Pumpkins! Pumpkins!—three pice a pound!" The Brahman boy thought that he would do as the green-grocers did and when any one passed, he called out at the top of his voice, "Wisdom! Wisdom! All kinds! All prices!" At first the passersby could not make out what he meant. When they understood, they did not think of buying his wares. They crowded round his shop and laughed at him. "Who would buy wisdom," they cried, "especially from a lad like that?" But the Brahman boy did not mind them at all. He went on shouting at the top of his voice "Wisdom! Wisdom! All kinds! All prices!" For several days he made no money at all; but at last the whole city got to hear of the new shop and four or five passersby stopped and bought an anna or two worth of wisdom. He was thus rather better off than when he had been an unpaid clerk; but he knew that when the novelty wore off, he would get no more customers. Still he did not despair.

It so happened that a certain Nagar lived in that city. He was really very stupid; but he had inherited a large fortune from his father and so he thought himself very clever. Just to show off, he called his only son VIDHYA or LEARNING. But inspite of this grand name, the son was just as stupid as the father. One day Vidhya passed the Brahman boy's shop and heard him shout "Wisdom! Wisdom! All kinds! All prices!" So foolish was he, that he thought wisdom was a sort of vegetable. He first asked its price per pound. The Brahman boy said "I sell not by weight, but by quality." Vidhya then put two pice on the counter and said he would take half an anna's worth. The boy wrote on a piece of paper

"It is not wise to stand and watch two people fighting." He then tied the paper inside Vidhya's scarf and took the money. Vidhya went home and said to his father "I have bought some wisdom for two pice and it is tied inside my scarf. Let us undo the knot and look at it." His father did not understand, but undid the knot and finding the paper read "It is not wise to stand and watch two people fighting." He was very angry and said to his son "Well, you are a fool! Fancy paying two pice for this nonsense! Why, every one knows that it is not wise to stand and watch two people fighting." In a great rage the Nagar walked to the Brahman's shop and began to call out "Rogue! Thief! Cheat! you did my son out of his money, just because he was a foolish boy. Give me back the two pice, or I shall call the police!" The Brahman kept his temper and said quietly: "Why are you so angry about nothing? I did not make your son give me the two pice. He asked me to sell him so much wisdom and I did so. Give me back my wisdom and take back your money." At once the Nagar threw the paper at the Brahman and cried: "Now give me my money!" The Brahman said "No, I said I would give you back your money if you gave me back my wisdom. You only offer me the paper. If you want your two pice back, you must sign a document, binding your son never to abide by my advice and always to stand and watch people fighting." The passersby took the side of the Brahman boy. The Nagar signed the document and went away with his two pice, very pleased to get them back so cheaply.

Two or three months later each of the king's two queens sent her maid to buy her some groceries. They both went to the same grocer and both tried to buy the same article. As the grocer had only the one sample they began to quarrel so fiercely that the grocer in a fright took to his heels and ran out of the shop. But the two maids went on quarrelling. Just then Vidhya strolled up and saw the quarrel. Before meeting the Brahman boy he would have run away; for stupid though he was, he knew it was unsafe to stand and watch a fight especially between the two queens' maid servants. But he remembered the promise made by his father, so he went close up and watched. One of the maids noticed him and called on him to witness that the other maid had struck her. The other maid retorted that so far from giving blows, she had received any number of them; and she, too, called on Vidhya to be her witness. At last they separated and the maid servants and Vidhya went to their several homes.

The two maids went to their mistresses and exaggerated what had happened. The queens in turn became furious and sent their maids to complain to the king. At the same time each sent word to Vidhya that if he did not depose in favour of her maid servant he would be beheaded. Vidhya was very frightened and told his father. The two talked the matter over all that day and all the next night, but they could not find a way of escape. At last Vidhya said " Let us ask the Brahman boy, who sells wisdom; if he really has any to sell, he may help me out." As a last resort, the Nagar agreed and father and son went to the Brahman boy's shop and told him what had befallen Vidhya. The Brahman boy asked for a fee of Rs. 500. On getting the money, he told Vidhya to feign insanity and to pretend that he did not understand what the king asked him. Next day the king heard the case. The king questioned him closely, but no question would he answer. He merely gabbled all the time, until the king lost all patience and drove him out of the court room. Very pleased with himself, Vidhya ran home and to all whom he met he praised the wisdom of the Brahman boy, whose fame thus spread through the whole city.

The Nagar was at first delighted at his son's escape ; then he began to reflect that his son must always feign insanity or the king would learn that he had been tricked and would certainly cut Vidhya's head off. He went to the Brahman boy, who asked for another fee of Rs. 500 which the Nagar paid. " Vidhya should go to the king," said the Brahman boy, " when he is in a merry mood and tell him the whole story. When he is in a good temper, he will laugh at it and forgive him." Vidhya followed the advice and one day finding the king in a good humour he confessed everything. The king laughed heartily and forgave him. Then he sent for the Brahman boy and asked him whether he would sell him wisdom and, if so, at what price. "Yes," said the boy, " I shall be very proud to sell the king wisdom ; but my fee will be one lakh." The king paid the lakh and got in return a paper on which the boy had written: "Do nothing without thinking deeply first." The king knew the advice to be excellent and dismissing the young Brahman, he had the words embroidered on all his clothes and engraved on all his plates, cups and dishes.

A few months later the king fell very ill. The prime minister eager to get rid of him, urged the doctor to put poison in the royal medicine. The doctor agreed and gave the king a poisoned draught. As the king lifted his gold cup to his lips, he saw engraved on it the words " Do nothing without thinking deeply first." Without suspecting anything he thought over the words and lowering the cup looked intently at its contents. The doctor's guilty conscience made him fear that the king guessed that the medicine was poisoned. He threw himself at his master's feet and confessing everything, prayed for mercy. The astonished king called the guard and had the doctor seized. He sent for the prime minister and bade him drink the poisoned medicine. The minister in his turn threw himself at the royal feet and begged for mercy. But the king had him hanged on the spot. He then sent for the doctor and after rating him soundly, banished him from the kingdom. Lastly he made the Brahman boy, whose wisdom had saved his life, Prime Minister and loaded him with honours.

GUZARAT FOLK STORIES—III.

MAGADHA AND RUPVATI.

Once upon a time there was a town called Avanti on the banks of the river Kshipra. It was a famous town and in it lived very many rich men. But all the inhabitants were not rich, some were very poor. Among the latter was a pious old Brahman called Vishnupriya or dear to the Lord Vishnu. He had two sons named Deval and Madhav. The former he married to a proud and lovely girl called Rupvati. For Madhav he got a pure and saintly girl called Magadha. In course of time the good old Brahman died and after his death the family became so poor that the two brothers resolved to leave Avanti and seek their fortune elsewhere. Before they left, they handed over the whole management of the house to Rupvati. Even Madhav said to Magadha in Rupvati's presence "You must obey Rupvati in everything. She is my elder brother's wife. You are but a foolish, ignorant girl. She is clever and wise in the ways of the world." Magadha was not vexed at what her husband said. She felt sure that what he ordered was for the best and she promised to do everything that Rupvati told her.

Now Rupvati for all her beauty was really a bad hearted woman and directly her husband had gone, she began to take as her lovers all the handsome young men of the neighbourhood. But she feared that Magadha would tell tales about her, so she resolved to turn her out of the house. She told Magadha that she had been born under an unlucky star and was the cause of her husband's and her brother's poverty. After rating her well, she beat her and pushing her into the street slammed the door in her face.

Poor Magadha was at first broken hearted at the way Rupvati had treated her. But after shedding some tears, she took courage and began to earn her living as a day labourer. From time to time, too, she used to go to Rupvati's house and work for her; for so gentle was her nature that she never bore Rupvati any ill-will. One day in Purshotam Mas she saw Rupvati worshipping the God Krishna. As she had never seen this done before, she asked Rupvati to tell her all about it. Rupvati flew into a temper and screamed at her "You wretched girl, fancy not knowing how to worship Shri Krishna! Why your very presence is a sin!" With these words she drove her sister-in-law into the street. As poor Magadha was going home in tears, she met one Bhamini, a friend of Rupvati and just as unkind and cruel as she was. Bhamini asked her why she cried. Magadha told her. But Bhamini instead of taking Magadha's part, thought it a good chance to play a cruel practical joke on her. She told her that it was Purshotam Mas and that therefore she should worship the God Krishna. "Most people," added Bhamini, "bathe in a river and burn a ghee lamp in a corner of their house in front of images of Krishna and Radha. Thereafter they feed Brahmans. But I know a much better way to worship Krishna than that. Choose the dirtiest, nastiest pool that you can find. Bathe in it and after bathing eat nothing but cold, stale food. Next worship the *pipal* tree, thinking all the while of Krishna and Radha. Then give to Brahmans alms wrapped in pipal leaves." Now this was all wrong; for Shri Krishna does not live in the pipal tree, which is only the abode of devils. But the cruel Bhamini hoped that in this way Magadha would incur both God's displeasure and the curses of the Brahmans.

Poor Magadha was far too trusting to guess Bhamini's wickedness and went home very pleased with her new knowledge. She looked about until she found a pool full of dirty rain water and swarming with water insects. She bathed in it, then worshipped a pipal tree, thinking all the while of Shri Krishna. Lastly she went home and ate some cold, stale food, which she had put by on purpose. Having done this for several days she invited 108 Brahmans to dine at her house. After she had invited them, she suddenly remembered that she had no money with which to buy them food, still less to give them alms afterwards. She did not know what to do, so she prayed all that night and all next morning to the God Krishna to help her honour the Brahmans when they came. A little before noon the 108 Brahmans began to collect outside Magadha's house. But poor Magadha, who had no dinner to give them, had not the heart to go to the door and welcome them; so she just stayed inside and prayed to the God Krishna. At last the Brahmans got very angry and said "What is the use of waiting outside this wretched little hut? Even if the door was opened, there would be nothing inside to eat." They were about to go away when three other Brahmans came up and one of them asked which was Magadha's house. Hopes of a good meal once more sprang up in the breasts of the 108 hungry guests and they pointed it out to the newcomers. "We are guests," they said,

" but she has shut her door in our faces. Are you her relative?" The Brahman who had spoken, said " Yes , I am Magadha's brother and these two are our kinsmen. Please wait outside and I shall go in and see. My sister must be getting ready your dinner." With these words he went inside the house, but he found nothing ready. In the middle room was poor Magadha, praying with all her might to the God Krishna to help her." " Why do you not serve the dinner for the 108 Brahmans ? " asked the newcomer. "There is no worse sin than to send away Brahmans hungry from your door." " I know that," replied poor Magadha, " but what can I do ? I have no food and no money to buy any." "Look in your kitchen," said the newcomer, " and you will find plenty of food." Magadha looked and sure enough the kitchen was as full as it could be. She was so pleased that she began cooking at once ; and two maid-servants, whom she had never seen before helped her and swept the floor of the dining room and got baths ready for the Brahmans ; when dinner was ready the newcomer called in the 108 other Brahmans and he and his two kinsmen served the dinner on leaves, which turned into gold plates when the guests touched them. The Brahmans had never eaten so rich or so big a dinner before. They got back their good spirits and instead of cursing poor Magadha, they blessed her from the bottom of their hearts. As they rose to go, the newcomer gave each guest a packet of pipal leaves as a parting present. The guests thought this a very odd " dakshina " but when they opened the leaves they found them full of diamonds and pearls and rubies.

When all the guests had left, Magadha begged the three Brahmans who had so wonderfully helped her, to have their meal also. They excused themselves, pleading that they had already eaten. But they pressed Magadha to eat and she did so.

Directly she had finished, her eyes were opened and she saw the three Brahmans and the two maid servants as they really were. For the Brahman, who had said he was her brother was none other than Shri Krishna himself and his two so called kinsmen were his two friends Uddhav and Akrur ; while the two maid servants were Shri Krishna's queens Rukmani and Satyabhama. Magadha threw herself at Shri Krishna's feet ; but the great God raised her and said "The ceremonies you performed in my honour were all wrong. But ceremonies are of little value. The true worth of worship is in faith ; and your faith was such that I granted you your prayers." With these words he took Magadha by the hand and led her back with him to his heaven Vaikunth. But what happened to the wicked Rupvati and Bhamini ? They were very properly punished. Rupvati in order to humble poor Magadha still more, had on the same day asked another 108 Brahmans to dinner, intending to give them a splendid feast and get their blessing, while poor Magadha fell under the curses of her 108 guests. But the very opposite happened. Rupvati cooked her dinner and had her house swept and garnished and went out to welcome her guests. But when she took them into her house there was nothing to eat at all. All the fine dinner which she had cooked for them had gone. She looked everywhere but she could not find it. At last she had to send the Brahmans away as hungry and cross as could be. As they went they called down the most frightful curses on her,so that she died soon afterwards and went straight to Hell. Nor did Bhamini fare any better. The God Krishna was very angry with her for telling Magadha to worship him in the way she did. She lost all her money and became very poor ; and when she died she went to Hell too, and she and Rupvati are still there, keeping each other company.

GUZARAT FOLK STORIES—IV.

RUPSINH AND THE QUEEN OF THE ANARDES.

Once upon a time there was a great king of Guzarat, who died leaving two sons Phulsinh and Rupsinh. On the father's death Phulsinh mounted the throne. In no long time he died leaving a widow and no children and Rupsinh became king of Guzarat, although still a little boy. Phulsinh's widow would have burnt herself on her husband's pyre had not the towns-people bidden her live and care for their child king.

The widowed queen was very wise and clever. So deft was she with her fingers that she could dress her hair with oil and afterwards press the hair so skilfully that not a drop of oil remained in it. One day when Rupsinh was a lad of fifteen, he lay asleep with his head resting on the lap of the queen. As he slept, she dressed his hair with oil and then began to squeeze it out. By chance she pulled out one of Rupsinh's hairs. Rupsinh awoke and said crossly: "You are not so clever to-day as usual with your fingers, or you would not have pulled out my hair." The queen said with a laugh: "Yes, I am getting old and make mistakes. If you want someone who will never make mistakes, you had better marry the queen of the Anardes." The queen was only joking, for the Anardes were a race of fairies. But Rupsinh took her words in earnest and cried "Marry the queen of the Anardes, then, I will! And till I have done so, I shall neither eat nor drink inside my king-dom." The poor queen regretted bitterly her words and begged the young king to pay no heed to them. But the headstrong boy would not mind her. He told his grooms, to saddle his horses. "Shew me," he said to the queen, "the house of the queen of the Anardes. If not, I shall seek her without your aid. I shall ask my way and with God's help I shall find it." The widowed queen was greatly grieved at the way the boy king had taken her words ; still, she thought it best now to help him on his way, rather than to thwart him.

She said : " If you will go, my King, then heed my words carefully, for the road is long and full of perils. Trust none whom you meet or you will perish miserably. On leaving the palace gates ride to the north. In three days' time you will come to a dense forest. Ride boldly into it and in its very heart you will find a lake. But beware of the lake and do not bathe in it or drink its waters. If you do, you will die ; for the lake is a fairies' lake and no mortal who bathes in it or drinks its waters can live. Ride therefore past the lake until you come to a great mountain. Avoid the mountain ; for near it lives a monstrous elephant ; and should it see you, it will trample you to death. Beyond the mountain you will come to Thugtown, a town full of thugs and cheats. They will kill you if they can. If you can outwit the men of Thugtown, you will come next to a beautiful wood. Here above all be on your guard, for the wood is peopled by demons who live on human flesh. Beyond the demon's wood lie the lands of the Princess Phulpancha. She is so called because her weight is only that of five flowers. In her country you will surely die ; but if someone will drop on your body three drops of Amrita, or ambrosia from the bottle that I give you, you will come back to life. Such are the perils that await you, yet if you still wish to go, take with you my blessing." As the widowed queen spoke, her voice trembled and the tears rolled down her cheeks, for she loved Rupsinh as if he had been her own son. She put in the youth's hands a bottle of Amrita. He took it, bowed his head to her feet, mounted his horse and spurring it along the northern road was soon out of sight.

Three days later Rupsinh saw, as he rode, the forest of which the widowed queen had spoken. He rode into it and rejoiced in the shade of the great trees overhead. Suddenly he saw in front of him, like a sheet of silver, a beautiful lake. Forgetting what the widowed queen had said, he let his horse walk to the edge and quench its thirst. A moment later he heard a noise of wings above him. He looked up and saw a great company of fairies on horseback flying towards the lake. The young king in a fright turned his horse's head towards the road and tried to spur it into a gallop. But the poison of the fairy lake was killing the poor horse and after trying feebly to answer to the spur, it fell down dead. The king undid the girths and taking with him the saddle ran to a big tree close by and climbed into its branches. The fairies had not seen him, so they dismounted; tied their horses to trees and plunged gaily into the fairy lake. Rupsinh slipped down from his tree and slipped noiselessly to where the queen of the fairies had tethered her horse and put his saddle on its back. He jumped on it and galloped off. The fairies did not notice their loss until they came out of the water. The queen was in great distress; and she and other fairies followed Rupsinh's tracks until they came near the elephant mountain. Far off they saw Rupsinh galloping away on the fairy queen's horse. They called to the elephant to stop him, as he was a horse thief. The elephant ran after the king and caught him and his horse in its mighty trunk. Carrying them to the mountain, it tried to crush them to death against one of its steep sides. The young king was in despair. Then regaining courage, he slashed so fiercely at the elephant's trunk with his sword that it let him and the horse go.

Rupsinh galloped away until he reached Thugtown. At its gate he saw an old man sitting. As the king rode up, the old man rose and with great courtesy said " Welcome, Thakor, Your father married you when a child to my daughter ; and yet you have never come to see her until now." " This is Thug-town." thought the king," and the old man must be one of the thugs who live there." Still Rupsinh could not but return the old man's greeting. He said " My father died so long ago that I cannot remember him at all, nor anything he did. It was only the other day that I heard from a kinsman that my father had married me to your daughter. I at once set out to claim my bride." The old man bade the king enter the town and stay at his house, that he might meet his daughter. They entered the town gates together. At the old man's door his four young sons came out and greeted the king as their brother-in-law. At night they would have led him to a room at the top of the house. But the king guessed that in the night they meant to throw him from the window. He said he could not sleep anywhere but on the ground floor. He was so obstinate that the old man at last put a bed for him in the verandah on the ground floor, while he and his sons slept in rooms off it. The king kept awake all night. It was well he did so. The queen of the fairies, who had never ceased to follow her horse's tracks, came to the old man's house and saw Rupsinh lying in the verandah. She tied a magic thread round his ankle and ran to the stable to mount the horse which the king had stolen. But Rupsinh untied the thread and tied it round the ankle of the old man. He had no sooner done so, than the magic thread became quite taut. The fairy queen had mounted her horse and riding off dragged the old man after her. She never thought of looking back, but galloped straight off to the elephant mountain. There she threw him before the elephant, who at once trampled the old man to death. In the meantime Rupsinh drew his sword. Going tc the beds of the four sons, he sternly demanded his horse. One of the four sons went to the stable to saddle it. As it was not there, Rupsinh made him give him one of the old man's own horses instead. He then rode as fast as he could out of Thug-town.

Rupsinh rode north for some hours when he saw in front of him a beautiful wood. He at once recalled the widowed queen's warning about the demons who lived in it. He entered it. Suddenly he saw two demons fighting together. When they saw the king they stopped fighting and began to laugh. Rupsinh laughed back and then asked them what amused them. "We have not tasted human flesh," said one of the demons, "for twelve years. When we saw you we laughed for joy. "But why did *you* laugh?" "I am a messenger of the god Shiva" said Rupsinh. "The parchment on one of his drums is torn and he sent me out to get two demon skins with which to repair it. The drum is so big that the skin of one demon would not be enough. So when I saw two demons in front of me, I laughed for joy." Rupsinh drew his sword and rode at the demons as if to skin them alive. In an agony of fear they begged him to take the skin of their blind uncle instead. "One demon's skin will not do," said the king sternly; "besides the skin of a blind demon would sound hollow." The demons in despair offered Rupsinh a large ransom, but he would not accept it. At last they offered him a flying machine known as a pavanpavdi. "In it," they said, "you can fly all over the sky and whenever you see a demon on earth, you can come down and skin him." The king took the pavanpavdi and tied it on to his horse's back and rode on until he crossed the borders of the Princess Phulpancha's country. Some time later he reached her town and lodged with an old woman who owned a garden outside the city.

The king had not been there many days before the princess came to hear of him. One day as he rode under her window her maidservants whispered to her, "That is the young king, my Princess." Phulpancha on the spot fell in love with him. One day Rupsinh came to his lodging, hungry and thirsty, and asked the old woman to cook him some food at once. The old woman said that she could not, as she was weaving garlands for the Princess Phulpancha. The king bade the old woman cook his dinner while he wove the garlands, which he did very skilfully. He then took off his diamond ring and hid it in one of them. When his dinner was ready, he ate it and the old woman went to the palace with the garlands. As the Princess put them round her neck, her fingers touched the diamond ring. She knew that it must have been sent to her by Rupsinh, as he lodged with the old woman. Some days later Rupsinh left his lodging and dressed as a poor Rajput, went to the court of Phulpancha's father and asked for service. The old king was pleased with Rupsinh's speech and bearing and made him chief of the guards round the Princess' palace and paid him three gold pieces a day. In this manner Rupsinh came to see the Princess almost daily and told her all about himself. Some days later came the weighing of the Princess Phulpancha. It was the custom of the land that once a year the Princess should be weighed on a pair of magic scales. If no man but the king had seen her during the previous year, her weight would only be that of five flowers. But if a man had seen her, her weight would be that of an ordinary girl of her age and height. At the appointed hour Phulpancha sat on one of the scales, while the weigher put five flowers on the other. Instead of the five flowers balancing the Princess, her scale clung obstinately to the ground; and it was not until two maunds had been put in the other, that the Princess began to move upwards. The old king made enquiries and came to know that Rupsinh had several times spoken to Phulpancha. Instantly he had Rupsinh hanged, from the branch of a tree. Fortunately before entering the king's service, Rupsinh had told the old woman of the garden about the Amrita. Hearing of the poor young king's execution, she went at night and sprinkled three drops of Amrita over his body. Rupsinh came to life again. But the old woman fearing the old king's anger would not take him back. Rupsinh was at first at his wit's end. Then he remembered the demons' pavanpavdi and seating himself in it he rose in the air and flew northwards.

After some time the young king came to a big garden in the midst of which was a palace seven stories high. He entered the palace and ran upstairs until he reached the seventh storey. On the top stair was seated an aged anchorite who said to him, "Welcome Rupsinh." The king was astonished that the anchorite should know his name and he asked the anchorite how he knew it. "My inner knowledge, my son, tells me your name. I also know that your brother's widow anxiously awaits your return. I know, too, that you are fated to win the queen of the Anardes." The king begged the anchorite to bless him. The anchorite did so and added, "To-morrow I shall go to bathe in a pool in the palace gardens. When I do sò, watch carefully the pomegranate trees in the orchard. You will see the pomegranates on them suddenly open and from each one will come out an Anarde. They will play and dance together in the garden and she to whom the others will pay deference is their queen. After a time they will go back to their hiding places. Note carefully the fruit which the queen enters. Then go down into the garden, pick it and take it back with you. But do not look behind you, as many others before you have done, or you will be turned into stone." Next morning the ascetic went to bathe and Rupsinh did as the ascetic had told him. He watched the pomegranate trees and soon from each fruit there dropped to the earth a tiny fairy. One of them, slightly bigger than the others, was clearly their queen. They played and danced for a time. Then they ran back to their hiding places. The pomegranates closed and hid their fairy lodgers from view. The king, however, had seen which pomegranate held the queen. He went into the garden plucked the fruit and turned back to the palace. Voices all round him cried out, "Strike him! Kill him!" But remembering the anchorite's words, he never once looked round until he had reached the palace door. Then he turned and saw the anchorite trying to soothe the other Anardes, for it was their voices which the king had heard. "It was fated that one of you should wed a mortal. What has fated has happened. So cease from troubling the king and his bride and give them your blessing instead." When he had calmed the fairies, he went to the king and said, "My son, start at once homewards and tarry nowhere on the road. Shew the pomegranate to no one until you reach your city."

The king mounted his horse without delay and started on his homeward journey. In no long time he saw an ascetic, who for 700 years had been doing penances, in order to win the queen of the Anardes. The king saluted the anchorite, who asked him whether he had won his goal. The king foolishly shewed the anchorite the pomegranate and let him take it in his hand. The sage put it under his foot and when Rupsinh asked for it back, sternly bade the prince begone. The king grew angry and threatened to take it back by force. The anchorite turned towards a big tree close by and consumed it with a single fiery breath. He then said to the youth with a mocking laugh:

"When I can blast a tree with a single breath, do you think that I fear you for all your valour? For 700 years I have sought to win the queen of the Anardes. I shall not give her up." But seeing how downcast Rupsinh looked, he gave him a wand and said "This is a magic wand. Take it. It will beat anyone whom you hate or fear and in battle it will always give you victory." The king took the wand, although he thought it a poor exchange for the queen of the Anardes, and going sadly to his horse got ready to mount it. As he put his foot in the stirrup, the wand spoke to him with a human voice, "O King, you do not know my name. It is Lalia Lath. For 700 years I have faithfully served the anchorite and now he has given me away in exchange for a woman. If you bid me I will give my old master a sound beating." Rupsinh, who felt very cross with the anchorite for stealing the queen of the Anardes, was delighted and said "Yes, give him a beating, the sounder the better." The wand then flew from the king's hand and began mercilessly to belabour the old sage, until in his pain and fear he threw away the pomegranate and begged for mercy.

The king picked up the fruit and with it the wand and he resumed his journey. Several days later he reached his capital. There he took out of the pomegranate the queen of the Anardes, who had by this time become reconciled to marrying Rupsinh. After greeting his sister-in-law, the widowed queen, he began to make everything ready for his marriage to the fairy queen; and in due time their wedding was celebrated with the greatest pomp and splendour. Unhappily in the crowd that watched the wedding was a pretty sweeper girl, called Rukhi and deeply skilled in black magic. She fell in love with the young king's handsome face and was filled with jealous rage at the happy look on the face of the queen of the Anardes. She devised a cruel plot, to kill her. She sought and obtained service in the palace, where the fairy queen shewed her the greatest kindness. One day the king, weary with the chase, fell asleep. The fairy queen had to go to a neighbouring well, to fetch water for her bath. She did not like to leave the king alone, so she asked Rukhi to watch by him until she came back. Rukhi promised to do so, but a minute or so later she followed her mistress to the well and pushed her in. Then she returned to the palace and by her magic made the king believe that she was the queen of the Anardes. But she could not so deceive the widowed queen. One day the latter in open durbar challenged Rukhi to go back inside the pomegranate. But Rukhi was too clever to be caught. She answered with ready wit: "I can no longer do that, sister, now that I am wedded to a mortal." She then complained to the king that the widowed queen always tried to vex her. So Rupsinh quarrelled with his sister-in-law and drove her out of the palace.

Now out of the well into which the fairy queen had fallen, there grew a most beautiful lotus. The gardener picked it and gave it to the king, who in turn gave it to Rukhi. The latter by her magic knew that the lotus had sprung from the body of the Anarde queen. She pulled off all its petals and threw it out of the window. The flower fell into a bed of soft earth and in a month or two there had sprung up a splendid mango tree that bore delicious fruit. Rukhi had the tree cut down but before it was felled, a bania had picked one of the mangoes and given it to his wife to eat. A year later she bore him a beautiful little baby girl. As the little girl grew up, she became the living image of the queen of the Anardes.

Rukhi guessed that she must have sprung from the mango, which had sprung from the lotus that had grown in the well, where the poor queen had been drowned. Rukhi began to complain of a bad pain and told the king that she had been bewitched by the bania girl and would not get well while the girl lived. The king had the bania girl hanged outside the eastern gate of his city. Another marvel then happened. The girl's head changed into an image of the God Shiva and her body into an image of the Goddess Parvati. Her right eye turned into a cock sparrow and her left eye into a hen sparrow. Her two legs turned into two plantain trees. When Rukhi heard of this, she got terribly afraid that the king would pass that way and see what had occurred. She told him never to pass by the eastern gate or the spirit of the witch girl would possess him. The king did not pass that way for a long time; but one day his horse ran away with him and took him to the eastern gate. He saw there a noble temple to the God Shiva. He went inside to pray.

As he prayed, he heard the hen sparrow say to her mate: "The king of this city is a fool" and thereupon she told the cock sparrow the whole tale of the queen of the Anardes. "This very night," continued the hen sparrow "the queen will come out of one of the plantain trees, into which the bania girl's legs have changed. She will worship the God Shiva, re-enter the plantain stem and never again be seen on earth The king heard the story and resolved to stay there all night. He did so and at midnight he saw one of the plantain stem open. Out of it came the queen of the Anardes. She began to pray to the God Shiva. Before she had ended her prayer, the king caught her by the hand. "Who are you?" cried the queen "and why do you take my hand?" "I am your husband Rupsinh," replied the king penitently. "I have been blind and cruel. But pray forgive me and I shall live with you always."

The queen was unwilling to stay, but Rupsinh held her firmly all night by the hand. Next morning the king's ministers and the widowed queen missing him, went in search of him. When they found him at the temple, the king told his sister-in-law all that had happened and begged her forgiveness also. The widowed queen, to test the story, shewed the pomegranate to the fairy queen and bade her hide herself inside it. She did so. The widowed queen called to her and she came out. The widowed queen had no longer any doubts. She buried the pomegranate in the earth and went back with the king into his city. There the king called together the townspeople and before them all repudiated the sweeper woman Rukhi. He then had her hanged on the very spot where the bania girl had been executed. After thus ridding himself of Rukhi, he sent for the Princess Phulpancha and married her as well as the queen of the Anardes. In their company and that of the widowed queen, the king lived happily for ever so many years afterwards.

ROUND ABOUT NASIK.

ROUND ABOUT NASIK.

The Nasik golf course with its many traps for the unwary, the club house with its friendly welcome, the dak bungalow embowered in trees are well known to the golf-loving Bombay resident. But there is another part of Nasik, its river, which is to him an unknown province. Yet pilgrims go there in thousands from all parts of the peninsula. Bones of dead men, who died a hundred leagues away are brought almost daily to be thrown into its waters. On its banks may be seen at any time young Brahmans practising *Prayanam* or breathing exercise or doing the *Achaman* rite, that is to say sipping water while repeating the name of some particular deity. There too may sometimes be seen the naked anchorite to whom the whole world stands in lieu of a garment; and he is not the least unhappy. As the Sanskrit verse has it "Courage is his father, Forgiveness is his mother, Tranquility is his wife; Truth is his son, Mercy is his sister, Self-restraint is his brother, Earth is his bed and the eight directions are his dwelling place." Let us therefore leave the golf course and the club house and wander together along the banks of the holy river.

In the first place how did the Godavari come to Nasik. Once upon a time the river Ganges was brought down from heaven by the austerities of King Bhagiratha of Ayodhya, so that he might perform the funeral rites of his kinsmen, the sixty thousand sons of King Sagar. To prevent the Ganges destroying the earth, the God Shiva caught her in his hair as she fell and kept her there for a whole year. Well the Ganges is a lady as well as a river and after some time Shiva's queen, Parvati, grew bitterly jealous of the fair woman, whom her husband carried continually in her hair. She consulted her son the elephant-headed Ganpati. That wise one found a solution for the difficulty. It so happened that at this time a *rishi* of extraordinary powers and merits named Gautama lived near what is now the bed of the Godavari river. To supply his limited needs he cultivated a little rice field. Ganpati turned himself into a cow and wandering towards Gautama's rice field began shamelessly to eat the holy man's scanty crop. Gautama, justly enraged, rose and with his staff admonished sharply the cow, that respected so little his sanctity. This was what Ganpati had foreseen. He fell dead on the spot. The news spread that Gautama had killed a cow. The neighbourhood was deeply shocked. Then through Parvati's and Ganpati's combined contrivance, the monsoon failed. The cause was clear. The *rishi* had killed a cow and the gods to punish him for this fearful sin had withheld the rains. The neighbours going in a body to the guilty *rishi* dilated on the sin that he had committed, until they had extracted from him a promise that he would by his austerities obtain water for their crops. Gautama to fulfil his promise went through the most incredible penances in honour of the God Shiva, until the latter asked the *rishi* what he wanted. " I want some of the Ganges water for the country side," replied the sage and he told Shiva the story of the sin which he had inadvertently committed. The God smiled as he heard the tale, because he guessed how it had come to pass. To humour his queen and at the same time to oblige the *rishi*, he released a part of the Ganges river at Trimbak and it became the Godavari. The neighbours of Gautama sowed their crops, the Ganges having lost the fairest portion of her waters lost half her beauty and Parvati ceased to be jealous.

Having brought the Godavari to Nasik let us next consider why Nasik rather than other spots along the river bank is so holy. The reason is that it was at Nasik that the hero King Rama of Ayodhya built his hermitage. The tale runs that his father King Dasharatha, urged thereto by his queen Kaikeyi, drove his eldest son Rama into exile, so that her son Bharata might succeed to the throne. The intrigue failed because Prince Bharata refused to oust his eldest brother. But Rama in order to abide by his father's words went with his brother Laxman, and his wife Sita, to live at Panchvati or Nasik. There they built themselves a hermitage and there Rama performed the funeral ceremonies of his father, when the latter died of grief at the loss of his son. It was there, too, that Laxman cut off the nose of a female demon called Surpanakha who fell in love with Rama and tried to kill Sita in the hope of winning Rama's undivided affections. Ravana, King of Ceylon, was the brother of Surpanakha and when his mutilated sister came shrieking to his court, he promised her that she should be avenged. To carry out this promise, he called in the aid of another demon named Maricha. The latter disguised himself as a deer with a golden hide and with horns glittering with precious stones. Sita attracted by the beautiful beast begged Rama to go and kill it and fetch her the hide and the horns. Rama agreed but before he went, he drew with his finger two long lines which together formed a sort of enclosure. " If you stay inside these two lines," he said to his wife, " no harm can come to you. If you stray beyond them, I shall not be able to protect you." Sita promised to stay within the two lines and Rama and Laxman went in pursuit of the golden deer. Instantly King Ravana who had been hovering in the sky inside his aerial car, descended to earth and assuming the form of a mendicant approached the hermitage of Sita and asked her for alms. Sita invited him to come to the door. But intending evil as he did, he could not cross the lines which Rama had drawn. So he answered haughtily that a religious mendicant did not run after alms. Those who wanted his blessings had to come to him. He accepted alms not as a favour received but as a favour conferred. The unsuspecting Sita unwilling to enrage the holy man went towards him, crossed the southern line and handed Ravana the alms. At once he reassumed his proper guise and seizing her by the hair threw her into his chariot and carried her off to his island kingdom of Lanka. The two lines are visible to this day and are known as the Aruna and Varuna streams.

The chief temple in Nasik is known as Kapileshwar. This is the story told of it. On one occasion the goddess Parvati for fun put her hands over her husband Shiva's eyes. But the great god was in no humour for fun. He opened his third eye and with it burnt up the sun, the earth and last but not least Brahmadev's fifth head. When Shiva had recovered his temper, he restored the sun and the earth, but he was not able to restore Brahmadev's fifth head. As a punishment for burning up another god's head, he was condemned always to see it dancing before his eyes. The punishment was a very severe one and to rid himself of the horrible vision, Shiva wandered all over India visiting in vain shrine after shrine. At last he came to the banks of the Godavari and sat down to rest under a tree. As he sat he overheard a conversation between a young bull and a staid old cow, its mother. "To-morrow," said the old cow, "our master will put a ring through your nose and yoking you to a plough will make you work for the rest of your life." "Indeed, he will do nothing of the kind," said the wicked young bull. "If he tries, I shall gore him to death." "O, you cannot gore him to death," said its mother deeply shocked. "He is a Brahman." "Never mind," said the abandoned young bull, "I know how to purify myself even from the deadly sin of Brahmahatya or Brahman murder." The God Shiva was greatly interested in this talk. He thought to himself that if the bull could purify itself from Brahman murder, he (Shiva) could, by doing what it did, purify himself from the sin of having burnt off one of Brahmadev's five heads. Next morning he returned to the spot, where he had heard the conversation. In a little time the Brahman came and tried to fasten the ring in the young bull's nose. The graceless beast threw him on his back and gored him to death. From being pure white, it became jet black with sin. However, it did not mind a bit, but galloping off with its tail in the air, plunged into the pool where Rama had performed the obsequies to his dead father. It became at once pure white, such was the holiness of the water. The tip of its tail, however, which it had held high in the air to shew its defiant spirit, remained black. The God Shiva watched the incident closely and immediately afterwards plunged also into the water. The same moment the ghastly vision which had haunted him disappeared. Close to the spot where these events happened was built the temple of Kapileshar or the god of the head. It is a temple to the God Shiva and commemorates his punishment and his release. It is the only temple in India where no bull kneels reverently in front of the God. For whereas in other spots the bull is regarded as Shiva's servant, here the bull is regarded as the great god's guru or teacher; for he taught the god to get rid of the vision that haunted him. Another fact proves the truth of the above story. Ever since, all white Deccan bulls have had black tips to their tails.

At a little distance from the river is a pool known as Indra's pool. The tale told about it is the following: Once upon a time there lived another great rishi also called Gautama. He had a charming and virtuous wife called Ahalya. Unfortunately her beauty caught the fleeting fancy of the God Indra,

He made to her certain improper proposals which she indignantly rejected. He then plotted with the moon to overcome her resistance. The moon rose two hours earlier than he (for the moon is masculine in India) should have done. Gautama anxious to worship the sun before he rose went to the river bank to bathe. The moment he went, Indra took his form and bade Ahalya rise and go with him. She thinking that it was her husband did as she was told. But just then Gautama detected the moon peeping over the horizon to see the fun. He at once ran back to the hermitage and caught Indra in the very act of going off with his wife. He held a summary trial, turned his wife into a stone, painted a black patch on the moon's face and made a thousand sores come on Indra's body. This state of things endured for several hundred years until one day King Rama's foot touched by accident the stone that had been Ahalya. She at once resumed her former shape. Rama took her to her husband and made him forgive her. The God Indra took courage at this and begged Gautama to forgive him too. The rishi turned his sores into eyes, but told him that, as he had behaved in a manner unbecoming a god, he never would be worshipped again. Indra went sadly away and at the *rishi's* command bathed in the pool of which I have spoken, and his sores all became eyes. But never since has he been worshipped in India. Lastly the moon begged for mercy. But the rishi would not abate a jot of his punishment and he wears a black smudge to this day.

When the wild Indian rains hide the hilltops and the plains—
  Teeming rain, steaming rain, blotting out the sky—
When the breakers leap and fall at the bidding of the squall,
  Then I think me of England, of England in July.
I wander in my dreams by her meadows and her streams—
  Olden streams, golden streams flowing towards the sea—
And I see their tiny billows as they lap against the willows,
  And the red rose is blowing—Ah ! 'tis there I would be.

* * *

But when Autumn with a sigh in December turns to die,
  She's a dark land, a stark land, grim and chill and grey.
When they lie the sodden leaves on the choking, dripping eaves
  And the window panes are blurred, then 'tis well to go away !
Yes, 'tis well to go away where there's sunshine all the day,
  Where down from the hills blows the dry, crisp wind,
Where one hears the wild duck whirring and one sees the rushes stirring
  And the hog deer's in the forests by the waterways of Sind !

* * *

Then she'll come across the brine, dear lady love of mine
  (Steamship, dreamship ! bring her safe again !)
And the white clouds above, they will greet my ladylove,
  And the blue skies will laugh as she speeds across the main.
And the great seas will roar on the gleaming Arab shore,
  (White rocks, bright rocks smile at her from me !)
While the trade wind blows, just to fan her as she goes,
  Till I see her kerchief waving as I stand upon the quay.